Moulis
Listrac

BERNARD GINESTET'S GUIDE
TO THE VINEYARDS OF FRANCE

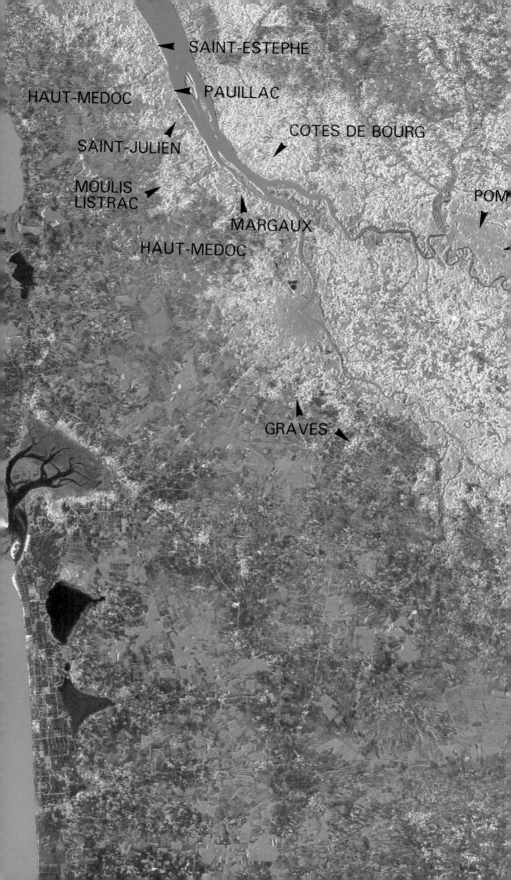

SAINT-ESTEPHE

PAUILLAC

HAUT-MEDOC

COTES DE BOURG

SAINT-JULIEN

MOULIS
LISTRAC

POM

MARGAUX

HAUT-MEDOC

GRAVES

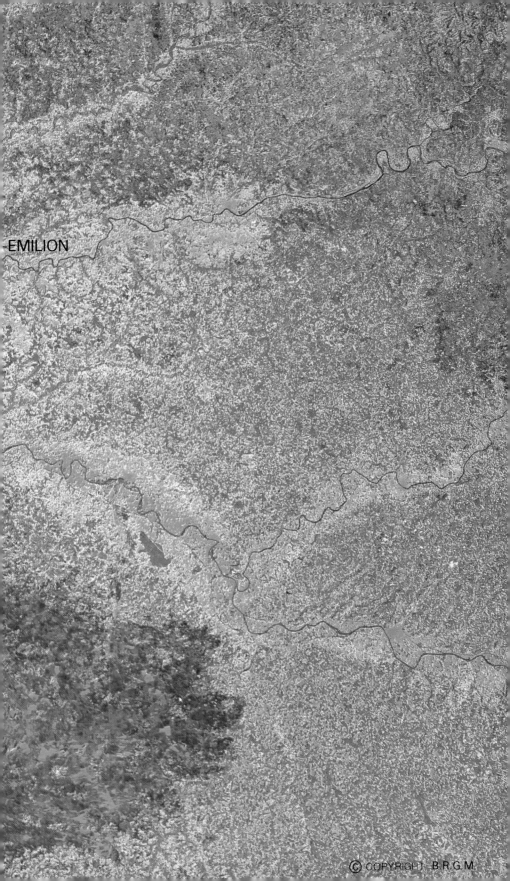

-EMILION

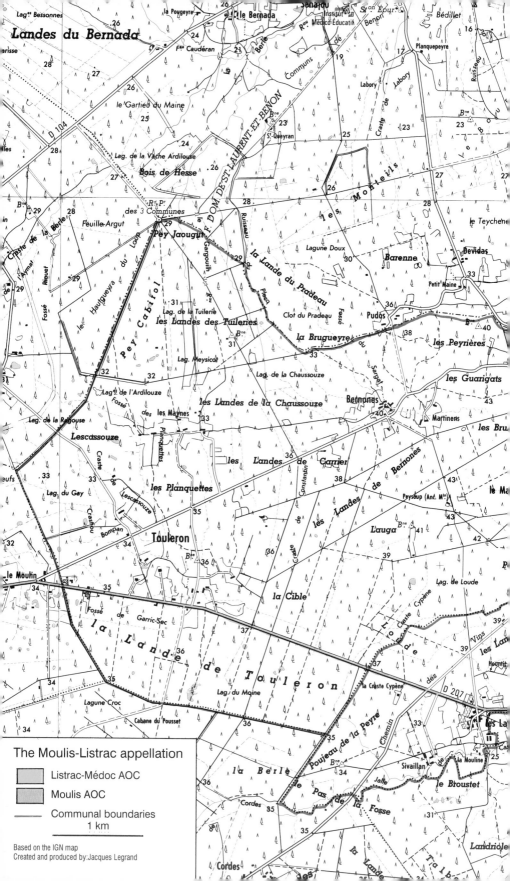

The Moulis-Listrac appellation

- Listrac-Médoc AOC
- Moulis AOC
- Communal boundaries
  1 km

Based on the IGN map
Created and produced by: Jacques Legrand

Didier Ters

Foreword by Nicolas Faith

Moulis
Listrac

Translated by John Meredith

BERNARD GINESTET'S GUIDE
TO THE VINEYARDS OF FRANCE

Jacques Legrand

Originated and produced by:

Jacques Legrand SA

English version edited by:

Editor:	Nicholas Faith
Assistant editor:	Tamara Thorgevsky
Translator:	John L. Meredith
Copy editor:	Barbara Mellor
Editorial secretary:	Christine Fourton
Art director:	Henri Marganne
Layout:	Claire Forgeot

ISBN 0-582-07541-6 for Longman UK distribution
ISBN 2-905969-40-7 for the rest of the world

Printed in Belgium by Brepols, Turnhout

Foreword

The late President Pompidou was the first French prime minister to order the wines of Listrac for official use. He was an appropriate buyer, the very embodiment of the rotund French bourgeois, appreciative of the good things of life, not overly pretentious – and with a keen eye for a bargain. The late lamented "Oncle Georges" and Moulis-Listrac were made for each other.

For these two villages, more than any other in the Médoc, are typical of the best of French rural life. They contain no great châteaux, and until the purchase of Château Clarke by Baron Edmond de Rothschild in 1973, there were none amongst the owners of the vineyards of the Médoc.

Refreshingly, they more resemble the many other agreeable vine-growing communities to be found scattered throughout rural France than they do the miserable, grey, feudal villages in the rest of the Médoc. Moulis and Listrac are living communities: it is no accident that Listrac's thriving cooperative was one of the first in the Gironde, a sure sign of a communal attempt to fight against the misery of the 1930s. They are well balanced agriculturally as well as socially, although in Moulis-Listrac we can never forget that the vineyards of the Médoc are merely clearings in the immense, oppressive, forbidding pine forests which cover the sandy dunes of the western two-thirds of what was for so long an isolated peninsula.

Didier Ters' book makes me feel guilty that I barely know the villages; it leaves me wanting to spend long summer afternoons amongst the vines listening to murmurous bees and dreaming about the wines I am going to drink that evening. For Ters knows the villages intimately and loves them dearly. His contribution to the series is particularly welcome because I am not alone in my ignorance. This is not surprising:

the villages lie between the two main roads along the peninsula, their vineyards often hidden in the woods.

The result is a profoundly traditional way of life, a peasant stubbornness – and eventual generosity – reflected in the sturdiness of the villages' wines, their refusal to please easily, or early, and the rewards they provide for the patient drinker. But traditional French rural habits are not necessarily ecological: every Médocain, certainly every male inhabitant of the two villages, feels he is born with a licence to shoot anything that flies, and Ters' description (on pages 42 to 44) of how the local diet was enlivened every autumn with thousands of larks trapped in nets as they migrated should put an immediate stop to any urban gush about the delights of rural life.

Fortunately the villages do not depend on larks for their livelihood. The story since the war is a welcome and familiar one, with growers' children returning from agricultural school eager to improve the family wine, and with a steady flow of small-scale, hard-working incomers, often returning from French North Africa, reinforcing the stubborn faith of the old-timers in the value of their wines. Their combined forces are now bringing back into production vineyards, large and small, whose capacity for producing good wine had been amply proved in the ninetheenth century, but which had subsequently been abandoned for several generations.

Nicholas Faith

Contents

By way of preface: A word about ageing

*I detest people who mouth about "nature"
without having any of it
in their hearts.*
Odilon Redon

This book, devoted to the appellations Moulis and Listrac, takes us on a complete tour of proprietors who, sometimes as the most recent in a long line of growers, sometimes as relative newcomers, produce excellent wines here in the heart of the Médoc. Thanks to his comprehensive knowledge of the region and its terrain, Didier Ters is a trustworthy guide. He overlooks no detail in order to guarantee his reader a thorough appreciation of the land, its vineyards and its people. But he goes beyond what we might call a "courtesy visit", for his stimulating style makes us want to know more. His commentaries on the wines are graphic sketches drawn with a vivid pen. And we find one common theme, a *leitmotif* – the need for ageing. In thus underlining what is more than just a tendency, Didier Ters draws attention to the innate virtue of the wines of Moulis and Listrac, an unquestionable virtue which they share with the majority of the great Médoc wines. Sometimes he appears to be rather hard on the philistines: "The example of Beaujolais Nouveau has created havoc even here in Bordeaux, and the wine is no sooner put in cask than the so-called experts are analysing it in abstruse language. True drinkers are not taken in and leave to the press the curious foible of wanting to describe what the man will be like before the infant is even born. Of course, business has its laws and practices, and publicity is one of them, but I say to the customer, 'Buy this wine and lay it down. Do not sabotage something that is still growing, needing several years to mature and harmonize five hundred constituent elements'."

It is true that in its thirst for the new and the instant our age often jumps the gun. It is true that the vast distribution system available nowadays cuts to the minimum the time that wine takes to reach the consumer, who thinks that in acting promptly he is acting for the best. It is true that many homes are victims of modern architecture and have not even a tiny area to lay down promising bottles. And yet

14

all these impatient people are depriving themselves of the pleasure of tasting a long-awaited vintage which has developed all its potential. Writing about a Moulis wine, Didier Ters declares: "It will always manage to have a future in front of it, even if the bottle is thirty years old." What a compliment! And how splendid for a wine still to be able to make plans at that age!

If I say that Didier Ters is an old friend, you will understand the fine nature of our friendship. And if he invites me to dine at his house, offering me an old bottle of wine, I know beforehand that it will be one of the best in his cellar. Wine and friendship are the two

"Vinissimo Grands Crus", an excellent wine cellar for people living in flats. Its outer walls are insulated and its feet absorb vibrations. It can hold 144 bottles. Without listing all its characteristics, it has four outstanding features:
1. The filtered double-glazed transparent door protects the wine from the light.
2. The temperature is regulated at about 12° C (53° F). The bottom, which is the coolest part, is ideal for white wine and champagne.
3. A humidifier ensures a constant humidity level of 75%.
4. The adjustable shelves are made of specially treated wood.
Moral: before investing your money and love in expensive bottles, be sure of being able to keep them properly. As the Médoc proverb goes: "There is no more wine without a cellar than there is money without a purse".

15

things in life which age well. You may with reason object that wine is not the only product of human industry to benefit from the passing of the years. This is of course so, but antiques, for example, do not change intrinsically as they age, whereas wine develops and moves towards its peak. And a great wine is undoubtedly the only work of art which can be drunk, all others being theoretically destined for posterity, or even immortality.

Moulis and Listrac are by nature areas devoted to tradition. This means that the growers are more conservative than elsewhere in their methods of cultivation, vinification and ageing. The vines too are maintained at a higher average age, and this has a very real effect on the quality of the harvest, the yields being much smaller. Fermentation is often done "à l'ancienne", over a longer period, allowing the natural elements contained in the grape-skins to penetrate deep into the wine, this being most obviously reflected in its colour. I have known a time when the "new wine" was drained off from the fermentation vats at the beginning of November, and then left in the cask for at least two years to allow it to improve with each racking. There were often two finings, sometimes even three. Modern oenology has changed these traditional practices at the same time as agronomy has improved the control of the condition of the vineyards. Today disasters are much less frequent than yesterday. But it is not the role of viticulture in the Médoc to produce wines for instant drinking. It is for this reason that they are inimitable and have been world-famous for centuries. Didier Ters is entirely right to insist on this important point, without which there can be no real understanding of wine. For although maceration is short today, the extraction of tannin is no less effective thanks to improved techniques in crushing and efficient temperature control. We may produce more supple wines than formerly, I agree, but not anaemic ones! The reduced time of ageing in the cask inevitably gives a lighter new wine. But it would be a gross error to imagine that after bottling the wine is a "finished product". An internal alchemy, still secret, will gradually modify the sum total of its organic and chemical parts, bringing about an ever-evolving natural balance.

There are different physical factors which can accelerate or retard a wine's ageing in bottle. The main one is temperature, but there are also vibration and humidity which, if excessive or insufficient, can affect the cork. Other more or less mysterious factors can also have an effect. For example, micro-radioactivity is a little-known phenomenon and its effects are difficult to calculate. We know that certain cellars constructed in the sand not far from the sea help wine to age more rapidly than those built in rock. Whatever the case, a good cellar should be free from vibration, have as constant a temperature as possible, between 12° and 14° C (54° to 57° F), and a humidity level of 70%. For those who live in flats, there are different types of storage cupboards which are perfectly suitable for keeping precious bottles. To conclude, I would say that wines stocked in unfavourable conditions do not age more quickly; they age badly!

One further question about ageing concerns decanting. When should we decant a great Bordeaux wine? My personal opinion is "always". For an old wine, the main purpose of decanting into a carafe is to separate the lees, so that we have a limpid wine in our glass. This deposit should be considered as the most natural of phenomena and not an irritating nuisance. For a ten-year-old wine, sometimes less, a deposit is reassuring. But it is not pretentious to decant a younger wine. Allowing a short time for breathing before serving can only be beneficial.

It is now time to follow our guide and discover these splendid areas belonging to the incomparable peninsula of the Médoc.

Bernard Ginestet

Living together, Médoc style

Once upon a time there were two villages, with two resonant names reminiscent of the old provinces of southern France, names you could roll round your tongue – Moulis and Listrac. They did not produce the excellent wines every year which are now responsible for their fame; they were simply two little areas in the country, just like any others; two church steeples in the middle of a classically agricultural, gently undulating landscape; two peaceful communes of France where you could find pure air and peasant stock in abundance. But because the wine is good, it has affected these glib clichés. Since 1938 in the case of Moulis and 1957 for Listrac, their two names have been linked with two wine appellations. A sort of second identity has superimposed itself on the first, confirming merits already recognized a hundred years previously, but, above all giving new life. This recognition and appreciation of their worth were both particularly welcome, for it should not be forgotten that Moulis and Listrac were overlooked in the 1855 classification of the wines of the Médoc. Protests have frequently been made since, complaining of the injustice. Way back in 1866, the notary Bigeat wrote hopefully, "the classification of the wines of Moulis is merely a matter of time". Vain hope. Only the unofficial classification of 1961 admitted four Moulis estates, situated on the remarkable terrain of Grand-Poujeaux's Garonne gravel, into the ultra-select club of the *crus classés* of the Médoc. But this was never confirmed; so Moulis-Listrac still waits in the wings.

Did the habit of linking Moulis and Listrac together come about because of this misfortune? It is not impossible. But geographically

◄ *A classic landscape of vineyards with a church steeple in the background. In several places, the forest borders the vineyards.*

everything already favoured this union. The two are neighbours, lying side by side. Their vineyards border each other and are even so closely interwoven (of which more later) that the châteaux of Listrac have vines in Moulis and vice versa. In some respects the boundary is vague and both communes participate in certain local events. For example, the local football team sports the colours of both villages. And again there is the official yearly recognition of the appellation for each *cru*, a ceremony which confirms the high quality of the wines of the appellation with an official certificate of recognition issued by impartial tasters (brokers, merchants and growers), based on blind tastings. This ceremony is conducted jointly, sometimes in Listrac, sometimes in Moulis. All the producers then lunch together and each drinks the wine of his neighbour. In his heart of hearts, he finds his own wine better, but he does not say so. Moreover, chauvinism in moderation is considered a virtue here. Although everybody prefers his own wine, he does not mind casting an eye, or rather a nose, over that of the others, just out of curiosity. It is all part of the local gossip: people like to know what is what. So they taste: "Well, well. Jean-Claude's 83 is very good. – Yes, but he bought new casks. – His father made good wine before him. I remember a 45... – Yes but all the same, with new wood, you can say what you like. – Well, I'll tell you what: new wood is all well and good for the Grands Crus. But at two hundred quid a cask, I'd have to get another bank loan. And you know, too much new wood's not good. The other day, I drank an 85. You'd have thought you were chewing a beam of oak..." The two communes are also linked together for the official price quotations: once a week, the brokers in Bordeaux announce the average price per *tonneau* for each appellation, calculated from the transactions recorded. For many years Moulis and Listrac have commanded the same price, so they share the rises or falls in the market, especially for bulk sales, without any jealousy arising from this healthy equality.

The two are also linked in a way which does not always please them, both being thought of as the two "little" appellations as regards size and the number of producers. They also both lie at a distance from what is known as the "châteaux road", the D2 which runs along the estuary, unfailingly leading visitors towards the neighbouring, yet rival, appellations of Margaux, Pauillac or Saint-Julien. Of course the village of Listrac is crossed by the *route nationale* from Bordeaux to Le Verdon, much used by the vast influx of tourists from all over Europe. And the Grand Listrac *cave coopérative* is well placed at the side of this road, once a Roman way. But it does not have the prestige of "the others". As for Moulis, both village and vineyards are firmly wedged between the two. No broad road leads the crowds of sunburned holidaymakers to the shade of the cellars. A great pity, and Moulis should publicize itself more to attract a clientele which at present is passing it by to the east and the west. The growers of Moulis have tolerated this misfortune with patience, but from time to time they reproach the Almighty a little for having deprived them of main roads and for having sandwiched them in. But they should comfort themselves, for everybody knows that the best part of a sandwich is what lies hidden in the middle.

They also share one railway station, with the name of Moulis-Listrac, which serves both villages, although it is in Moulis, at Grand-Poujeaux. Trains came to Moulis for the first time on July 24, 1869, four months after their celebrated arrival in Margaux. Moulis was a halt planned by the Médoc Railway Company on the Bordeaux-Le Verdon line, but the engineers responsible for its construction certainly had no idea of the importance it was to assume in the twentieth century. It partly enabled Listrac's *cave coopérative* to supply the railway company's dining-cars. Of course, the quality and price of the wine played an important part, but the proximity of this station ensured easy, rapid and cheap transport, particularly with the use of tank-wagons specially designed for wine. Between 1950 and 1960, thousands of hectolitres were dispatched from this tiny station, destined exclusively for the use of the railways.

But the *coopérative* was not the sole user. For a long time (and still today), the local growers dispatched their products by rail. It is still not uncommon to see the waiting-room full of handsome wooden boxes, stamped with famous names. Twenty-five years ago, Maucaillou's wine was brought by horse in a sort of "coffer" containing six hundred bottles, packed in boxes of thirty. This system is no longer in use – doubtless because there are no more horses. But the railway's traditions still remain. A short time ago, a traveller got out at Moulis-Listrac station wanting some precise, rather important information. The station master was full of good intentions but was unable to supply the exact details to satisfy the enquirer. So he had to telephone the regional head-office in Bordeaux. He did so, but not before changing his cap, putting on his newest and finest for the duration of the call, and standing to attention. This was how a civil servant should address his superiors! (This story is absolutely true).

But although there are many points in common between the two villages, each commune has always retained its independence and personality. Wine is the best witness to this and is undoubtedly partly   23

TALUS AND RESIDUAL DEPOSITS

| RD | Residual or Aeolian deposits Sand and silt |

| CFy | Gravel and coarse sand with clay |

ALLUVIAL FORMATIONS

| Fyb | Clay and recent sand |

| FXb1 | Sand and gravel with pebbles |

| FXb | Gravel and sand |

OLIGOCENE DEPOSITS

| g2A | Marine asteroidian limestone |

| g1C g1S | Marls and lacustrine limestone |

EOCENE DEPOSITS

| e7a 2E e7bS e7bC | Marine limestone |

| e7bR e7a1 | Marls and clay |

| e6a e6b | Clay and lacustrine Plassac limestone |

| e5c | Limestone and Listrac marls |

Scale 1:50,000

©IGN - BRGM - J. Legrand

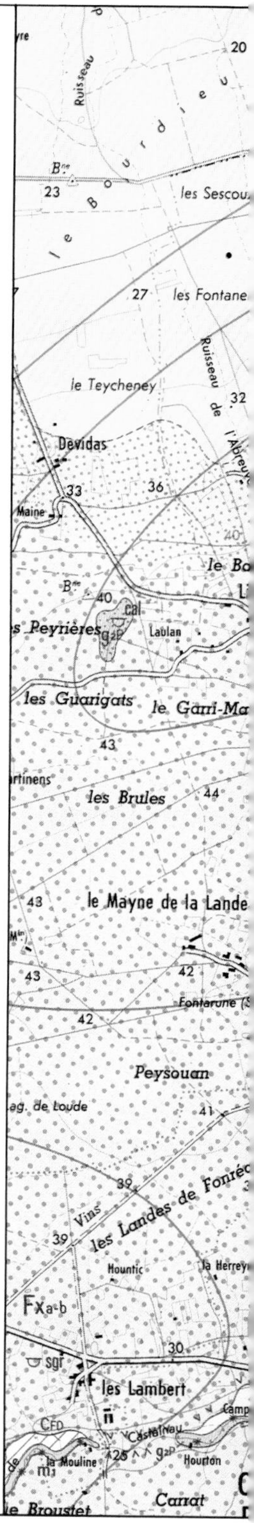

24

responsible. Geology appears to be the cause of this individuality. Generally speaking the soil of Listrac is clayey limestone, which give the wines more vitality and body. This robust constitution makes Listracs the most full-bodied wines in the Médoc, together with certain Saint-Estèphes. There is a typical Listrac, and we shall speak of this again. On the other hand, the best land in Moulis, at Grand-Poujeaux, is exclusively of gravel. Without this area, the appellation would never have achieved its fame. It is a slope of Quaternary pebbles stretching over some 150 hectares, producing wines distinguished by the cabernet grape and a poor soil. They differ from those of Listrac in having a lighter, but more elegant, constitution. Listrac wines are not better than those of Moulis; they are different. We can compare them, but appreciating their qualities is simply a matter of taste. Consumers have long since settled the problem: they like them both, which keeps everyone happy.

The distinction in the flavour of the wines from the two appellations is very fine indeed. Blind tastings, even those organized by experienced tasters, sometimes give such unexpected results that we should be wary of preconceived ideas. There are gravelly soils at Listrac, such as those of Médrac, producing wines which inevitably resemble those from Grand-Poujeaux. And there are vines in Moulis entirely on clayey limestone whose wines resemble those of Listrac. This creates a certain confusion which secretly maintains the relationship between the two. Château Clarke may be in Listrac, but a tenth of its vines are in Moulis. And Château Maucaillou may be in Moulis, but it harvests in the Listrac appellation, and even at Lamarque in the Haut-Médoc. This being so, how can one be precise about the difference in type between the two appellations?

It is more rewarding to try to determine their nature in relation to other comparable Médoc appellations. Of the communal appellations, Moulis and Listrac are the furthest inland; they are furthest away from the river and nearest to the forests. This is why they are rather "out of the way", as we mentioned before. But they are also out of the way of the mists which rise along the estuary. This means that overall the vineyards are in better condition, for the grapes suffer less from rot. It also means that harvesting can sometimes begin later than elsewhere, with no risk of mould. Although rot is "noble" in Sauternes, so noble that it is indispensable for the fabulous

Growers view snow as a good pest deterrent.   ▶

Part of a grower's job is to renew parcels regularly. It is easier for large vineyards to maintain vines at a constant age.

wines it produces, it is an enemy to be feared among black grape vines. Moulis and Listrac have less of a struggle than the growers who "look out over the river". Is it this healthy condition which gives a consistency which is quite remarkable here? It is not impossible. It is clear that, by comparison with the irregularities in the vintages elsewhere, the *crus* here are privileged in producing wines of a stable quality. Where others have failed, Moulis and Listrac have been successful. So the years 1973, 1974 and 1977, which were very uneven in the Médoc, produced wines here which are sometimes magnificent. Of course, the sixty or so growers in the two communes did not all reach the heights, but the proportion of those who made wines which, without any exaggeration, are delicious to drink today is higher than the average for the Médoc.

On the other hand, as if there were some hidden force needed to compensate for this, cold causes much more damage in Moulis and Listrac than anywhere else. In January 1985, during the two nights in which the temperature dropped to minus 20° C (-68° F), some one hundred hectares of vines froze in Listrac. Two-thirds had to be uprooted. Of course the vineyards in Moulis have also had their share of disasters. The grower fears winter frosts, much more than hail or spring frosts because unlike hail, against which everyone is insured, there is no compensation for winter frosts, which can destroy a vineyard's production, not only for one harvest but for five or six, because new vines have to be replanted. Even if the plant has not been uprooted and there is just hope that it might take again, it will still bear the scars of the cold for several years, giving only a moderate yield or growing at a slower pace. In 1985, a harsh frost caused damage estimated at 1.4 million francs in the vineyards of Listrac. That is a heavy loss. Again, during the winter of 1986 and 1987, the growers watched anxiously as both snow and temperature started to fall at the same time. They could not help remembering that Monday morning in February 1956 when they woke up to find their land three feet deep in snow. However attractive, however magnificent was the blanket of white, it was a horrible sight to the people of Moulis-Listrac: the vines were frozen to the roots. We would have to go right back to the time of phylloxera to find such serious damage. Indeed, it was so extensive that whole estates were abandoned. The Moulis vineyards, which had a total size of some 370 hectares in 1955, were progressively reduced to 280 in 1962. And yet 62 was a good year for the wine. Today, out of the commune's total area of 2,000 hectares, 500, or a quarter, are under vines. But it still remains the smallest appellation in the Médoc – smallest, that is, in size.

During the last twenty years the vineyards of Moulis and Listrac have developed considerably both in size and, incontestably, in quality. Less subject to the caprices of fashion, snobbery and speculation, they have gradually and patiently ploughed their own furrow. They have penetrated the *crus bourgeois* league, which says a great deal. Take the results of the various Coupes des Bourgeois du Médoc, organized by Gault et Millau and other professional bodies. Each time there was a Moulis or a Listrac among the first three. Even better, Maucaillou won in 1986. The awards list is important, because three vintages of each *cru* are tasted. This is a sound method of forming an opinion about a wine. In the face of other appellations, perhaps more used to wearing laurels won earlier, the progress made here is spectacular. One further proof is the result of the official classification of the 1986 vintage. For a total Listrac harvest of 30,000 hectolitres with the right to the appellation, only some 116 hectolitres were refused, representing the production of 3 hectares out of 530. This was the first time that such a negligible proportion had been rejected and will go down in history as a sort of record for viticulture in Listrac. Merchants would be well advised to visit the area. They will find sound wines (like the people who make them), well-kept estates, modern vat-houses, cellars with more and more new casks and surprisingly modest ex-château prices. This general improvement in Moulis and Listrac, rather like that of the wines in the Bas Médoc (which have been underestimated for too long), is the most important feature of these vineyards today. It is time to reflect that there are no longer any minor appellations in the Médoc.

From larks to mushrooms

Roughly speaking, Moulis and Listrac represent one thousand hectares of vines. So the two communes together have less than Margaux or Saint-Estèphe but about the same as Pauillac. One thousand hectares, compared with Clos de Vougeot's sixty-five, is obviously considerable. But in relation to the eighty thousand hectares which make up the two communes, it also leaves space for meadows, woods, gardens, other crops and the pine forests. This is important if we want to understand the traditional way of life to be found here. Obviously more land could be planted with vines, but then, what would become of those oak forests, so precious in autumn when, at the end of the harvest, the vigneron takes his stick and his dog and goes looking for cep mushrooms among the ferns? And what about those chanterelle omelettes, so eagerly looked forward to every year, which mark out the rhythm of the changing seasons? If we look more carefully at the countryside of Listrac and Moulis, we see it is infinitely more wooded and varied than that of the other Médoc appellations. It is quite common to come across a herd of cows or sheep, or to have to brake suddenly because a hen is crossing the road with her brood, or to see a billy-goat with its splendid horns whispering sweet nothings to some other pretty goat from the neighbourhood. In fact, all sorts of crops are grown here, and vines do not have a monopoly. Even at Château Clarke, Baron Edmond de Rothschild insisted on having a kitchen garden, for he found that home-grown potatoes tasted better than those from the supermarket. This was not just a millionaire's caprice; unconsciously, the Baron has fallen into line with the rest of the village. All he needs now is a poultry-yard to become permanently integrated.

Along with mushrooming, shooting and fishing play an important role in day-to-day life. They are both long-established traditions, a legacy handed down to everybody, and a sort of right which must be exercised so as not to betray those who have passed it on from time

The primary role of the acacia in the Médoc is to supply vine support-stakes, but its flowers, hanging in racemes like bunches of grapes, encourage bee-keeping and give a deliciously sweet honey.

immemorial. Each season has its customs. The arrival of shad and elvers in the estuary mobilizes all those who have the good luck to own a little boat in the port at Lamarque or round about. As soon as the arrival of these river migrators is announced, nets are ready, and sometimes work in the cellars is delayed. That does not matter for, by definition, wine can wait, whereas the fish will not be there for long. Shad, like steak, is cooked on a fire of vine-prunings with sorrel (home-grown, if possible). It is a great treat, provided your eyes are sharp enough to spot the hair-fine bones. You need a good white wine to go with it – a Saransot-Dupré would be ideal. This is the only white wine marketed in the whole of Listrac and Moulis, until Château Clarke starts to sell again its excellent and once very famous Merle-Blanc.

The grower is also a hunter. In November, among the vine-rows where there are still grapes which have been overlooked by the pickers, he watches out for thrushes coming to feast on them. The Médoc hunters are particularly fond of this bird, for it should be cooked with grapes and eaten with a bottle of old wine. There is deer-hunting too, though this is done in parties. Deer are so numerous in the huge forests, where they are rarely disturbed, that the communes authorize the cull of a certain number every year. So on one or two Sundays, hunters gather together with their guns, dogs and refreshments – for it should be stated forthwith that these hunts are celebrated with plenty of good wine. They start in the morning, but at midday, whether a deer has been taken or not, the hunters call a halt and turn their attention to more serious matters. They have brought along bundles of vine-prunings for the fire, meat in large quantities, and as many bottles as necessary to celebrate the occasion in suitable style. Then they sit down at table. In this atmosphere of ritual and festivity, the taking of a deer, a perfectly innocent victim unjustly accused of eating the young pine-shoots, seems to be a way of making an expiatory sacrifice. This hunter's feast recalls how ancient civilizations sacrificed whole flocks to prepare the people for great religious rites or general rejoicing. History has not left us any trace of the protests undoubtedly made by Greek, Roman or Egyptian ecologists of the time.

Banquet follows banquet. The one organized every year by the Viticultural Federation of Listrac is legendary. It generally takes place at the beginning of winter when fermentation, maceration and casking of the wine are all finished and, after a busy autumn, the vigneron can get his breath back and spend time with his friends. The occasion brings together some hundred people. The first wine of the

latest vintage is drunk as an aperitif. The mayor and local priest are present, sitting with the Federation's president at the head table and looking like carefully placed figurines in a Nativity scene. Everybody sits down at table at about eight o'clock in the evening expecting not to leave before one in the morning, because the evening is a dinner with entertainments. The dinner side is looked after by the chef of the Hôtel de France in Listrac, with a menu consisting of not less than six courses. In 1986, there was Henri IV soup, a seafood platter, fillet of sea-bass in Médoc wine, leg of lamb, cheeses and Grand Marnier soufflé. There were many different wines and, to accompany the various courses in the fashion the occasion demanded, people drank heartily. First there was a chilled rosé, followed by Clarke 83, Lestage 83, La Bécade 82, Gobinaud 82, Fourcas Hosten 79 and Grand Listrac 70. To save face, everybody had to drink at least two glasses of each. But that was not the end of it. After coffee, the survivors attacked the last round in the form of a spirit whose name cannot be translated into English. It is the famous "GN". Do not try to guess what this stands for. "GN" means *gnole-con*! I apologize to French-speakers for introducing an indecent word into this story but it would not be complete without the right vocabulary. In the style of the pure Girondin and the local Bordeluche, the man from the Médoc likes to punctuate his sentences with the word *con*, to emphasize what he is saying. So, *gnole-con* (whose first and last letters give the modest GN) is even better than eau-de-vie, in the primary sense that it is made here. You will find in it a truly local flavour. Monu-

---

▲ *The training of vines has developed considerably since the nineteenth century, but the vigneron still plays a vital part.*

ments have been given a preservation order for less. This eau-de-vie is made from grapes, and is "only" 48 per cent alcohol, no more. It has been kept for at least fifteen years in small new casks containing a few acacia cuttings. This strong spirit with its powerful bouquet will reconcile you with the Almighty if you are feeling melancholic.

As for the entertainment, this is provided by the growers themselves and is well worth seeing. It is a medley of theatre, song, music, cinema and particularly humour, clearly illustrating the gaiety of the world of wine. The theme for the 1986 show was the Olympic Games. This aimed at proving, with films to help, that Listrac was capable of organizing such an event! The sketches had been filmed in summer. The public wash-house had been turned into an Olympic swimming pool, the pools in the gravel quarries were used for regattas, the vines for hurdle-races, and some scenes were set in the municipal stadium. Of course, all the youngsters of Listrac wore Olympic gear for these different events. The results were just like the film – unrelatable, especially because the people watching the film were the actors themselves, their parents, neighbours, friends or other relations. More or less everybody is related in Listrac, and the Viticultural Federation is one big family both in the figurative and the literal sense of the term.

Towards the end of the evening there is another type of performance worth watching, for while some are dancing, others produce streamers and blowpipes and aim slyly at the mayor and the beaming, ruddy, contented faces of certain guests. Six courses and six wines eventually make their mark. From the *vin nouveau* to the GC, the drinking has been of marathon proportions and you have to have a solid constitution to stay the course. The young folk will not go to bed before five o'clock in the morning, but the older ones will leave long before they feel that sleep and wine have got the better of them. This is the moment when the chairs are pushed back, shirt collars are undone and old memories are relived. It is the time too for singing old songs of the *cru,* with lyrics which are sincere and comforting without being great poetry. Here is a verse from one of them:

> "Listrac village is in the Médoc,
> Famed for wine and for fine châteaux;
> Deeply proud of its choicest vine-stock,
> Cabernet, merlot and verdot."

It is not Verlaine, but it comes from the heart. Everyone takes up the chorus, sung to the tune of *Les Chevaliers de la Table Ronde.* Small growers who are members of the *coopérative* and owners of

big châteaux join together in this Bacchic revelry, singing lustily, with their glass in hand. But the glass tends to be empty: they have drained it.

It is a pleasure to pay tribute to this solidarity, which unites the *grands-bourgeois* and the *crus artisans* in good and difficult times alike. In Moulis, there are estates of 60 hectares; in Listrac, there is a château with 140 hectares. But there are also proprietors who own only a few rows, making wine for their personal consumption. For example, there is Simone Moreau, who has two thousand very old vines over in Médrac; or Hubert Roux, a policeman in Bordeaux,

▲ *The "Bouillie Bordelaise", invented a century ago, was the salvation of French vineyards. Above is one of the first spraying machines able to run between the rows of vines (Collection Château Maucaillou).*

who is happy to have 0.16 hectares of merlot in Listrac; there is the Lartigues family, producing four casks from old merlot vines for special family occasions; and the Vidalliers, with five thousand vines in Listrac, just about half a hectare, not giving enough wine to make bottling worthwhile. These growers with their micro-production are not on the list of "châteaux". But in their own way they carry on the tradition of the region, when formerly everyone had a few vines, a bit of forest land, some cattle and did a little farming. The crisis of the thirties killed this tradition. In the face of the general slump, parents advised their sons and daughters not to stay on the land or they would starve. "Join the police force. At least you will have something to put on your back", they would say to children they wanted to protect from poverty.

There have been hard times in the villages of the Médoc, and the visitor who sees them for the first time cannot have any idea of events even in the relatively recent past. By comparison with the days when to have half a pig was the height of luxury, the region is obviously now more prosperous. But the people who knew these hardships still remember austerity. This is what has helped them to turn the corner. You could say that difficult times made people harder and more resilient, for Listrac is an area of centenarians. Good wine, open air and the forests make for solid people. No one is surprised to see 90-year-old Marguerite Dubosc looking after her Château Lalande with all the energy of a woman of twenty. When Marie Guitard died at the age of 108, there was general stupefaction. As she had not been ill, everyone thought that she was still good for another ten years. And these are not isolated cases. The old people

make up an integral part of the landscape, but they often hand on

This turn-of-the-century postcard shows Moulis's gamekeeper watching a group of gleaners. Christian and Guy Videau are the last people in Listrac to bring their harvest to the cave *by horse. Bottom row, Jean Saumur, a great lover of larks, and Lucie Cressent, a local character.*

41

the torch to their successors rather early: that is at about eighty years of age! For then, they say, you cannot taste wine as you used to. Their sense of smell loses its keenness. So, as they cannot drink conscientiously, they have another pleasure – strawberries in wine. But not those awful huge strawberries, as big as quinces with flesh like cotton-wool. No, the little deep-red strawberries, very sweet, almost crisp and superbly juicy. Very slowly they cover them with a good measure of old wine, of a year which has not been sold. At the back of the cellar there is still a good number of bottles hidden away where the Germans could not find them. Take my word for it: these strawberries with a 1914 Moulis or a 1940 Listrac are something special. We should listen to the old folk more often.

Still on the subject of this traditional rural way of life, Moulis and Listrac still preserve a way of hunting which has almost disappeared elsewhere. It is with the *pante,* or lark-net. When other hunters are starting to shoot the ring-dove in the Landes or the Pyrenees, these men hunt in a different way, by stretching huge nets across the flat, open meadows which have been ploughed to expose the bare soil. The net, also called a "matole" or a "pandèle", is generally some twenty-five metres long by two metres wide. This type of hunting is very strictly controlled and, by law, the net must not exceed fifty square metres. The nets are always in pairs and are arranged flat on either side of the points where they are fixed. They are linked to springs hidden in the grass which the hunter can activate from a distance, by means of ropes, from his hiding place in the branches. At the beginning of November, when the east wind starts to sweep over the countryside, the larks arrive from the north in flocks of several hundred at a time. The hunter calls to them with a sort of high-pitched cooing to attract them. There are two larks already in the middle of the net, held prisoner by a string attached to their legs. They too attract their fellows and, if everything goes according to plan, the flock swoops down and settles. This is the moment to release the springs, and in an instant the two nets fold over each other, rather like double doors closing together. The next part is less sporting, for the larks have to be collected one by one and killed with a sharp pinch on the neck. Then the nets are stretched out again in the hope that another flock will come and settle.

One of the traditional methods of hunting in the Médoc, the pante, *belongs to a typically regional way of life. For the locals, nothing could be more delicious than a few of these little birds on a skewer, accompanied by a good bottle of Moulis or Listrac.*▶

At one time dozens and dozens of flocks were taken, but today this form of hunting is permitted for only three weeks in the year. Even game birds such as snipe or woodcock are less abundant than before, and larks are becoming rarer and rarer. Yet it is still common for a hunter to take two or three hundred birds in one season. This "pante" belongs to the traditional type of hunting of which the Médoc is so fond. From time to time, voices are raised in protest, demanding that it should be stopped because of the tremendous destruction of wild migratory fauna. Although shooting turtle-doves in spring is not easy to defend because of the basic laws of nature, the "lark-net" is a traditional practice which still deserves its place in the region. Like pigeon-shooting, it requires a lot of skill and expertise, and it belongs to a rural way of life, typical of the Médoc, which it would be a pity to lose.

And, when all said and done, larks are good to eat! They can be cooked in various ways – in a salmi, stewed with grapes, or roasted in the oven. In Moulis, they are plucked and gutted, then their beak is cut off and they are rolled in bacon and skewered four at a time before being grilled over a fire of vine-prunings. If this is to be an entrée, six will be enough, but if it is the main course you need fifteen, although that will still make only fifteen mouthfuls. You can use your fingers (indeed, you have to) and I recommend you uncork a good bottle. A Listrac 71 or a Moulis 76 would be perfect for feathered game.

Our forefathers the millers

Molis, Molys, Moulix, Moulinis – the spelling may vary but the etymological root is the same. The name of Moulis comes from the mills which were once so numerous here. This is not surprising. The Inventaire d'Aquitaine very recently conducted a scholarly study which revealed that in the canton of Castelnau alone, consisting of nineteen communes, no fewer than thirty-two watermills and fifty-six windmills – a total of eighty-eight – had been built over the centuries. In the whole of the Médoc at least four hundred mills are said to have been built, which is a large number for a region reputedly poor in agriculture, if we exclude vines. At Moulis the first mills were built on the "jalles", those little rivers which run across the countryside towards the estuary of the Gironde. Frequently narrow and hidden beneath the trees, they give the landscape a true note of paradise. The water is clear, the bed generally of light-coloured sand. Violets and primroses cluster along the banks in spring, and above them asphodels mingle with the broom in thick clusters. By comparison with the rows of vines, which are inevitably geometrically aligned, these clumps of wild flowers are like a miracle. But they are not obvious; you often have to spend some time seeking them out, which of course adds to their charm.

There are still three watermills at Moulis, though unfortunately not in use. The first and undoubtedly the oldest is that of Tiquetorte, first known by the name of Artiguetorte. It is said to have been constructed during the Hundred Years' War by the English themselves, or at least under their regime. It stands on the brook of the same name between Châteaux Brillette and Citran on the outskirts of Avensan. The second is that of Le Blanc, situated by the roadside between Bouqueyran and the village, and so called because it ground corn rather than rye, which gives a darker flour. The third is the mill known as La Mouline, on the little Castelnau river to the extreme south-west of Moulis in the forest of Les Lambert, which you

have to cross when you go to Carcans for a swim. Old maps give it various names: the mill of Gens, Cular or Broustay. Future maps might perhaps call it the Scouts' Mill because of the summer youth camps. Thanks to them, although the building has been put to another use, it is kept in perfect condition. Formerly, watermills were all equipped in the same way. The water was channelled downwards to give it some impetus and then ran through the arches built across the river. The wheel was under the mill. In the Middle Ages it generally had scoops hollowed out of very hard rowan wood. Later on there were cast-iron bowls, a sign of progress. But the mechanism was still the same; as it turned, the wheel started the millstone, which in its turn rotated on the millstone and ground the corn.

It seems that the windmill came later and it is likely that the Dutch, who came during the seventeenth century to drain the marshes of the Médoc, increased their number. There are a few remains at Listrac as well as at Moulis, but only in the form of topless round towers, probably dating from the eighteenth century. It is interesting to note that a windmill is often to be found close to a watermill, replacing it in times of drought or flood when the river was useless. Aeolus replaces Neptune at a moment's notice. This precaution, typical of the ingenuity of country life in former days, shows just how important bread was - even more important because the mills

---

▲ *Moulis owes its name to the numerous mills on the brooks arriving from the plains of the Médoc.* ▶

46

were then what the "cafés du commerce" are today. People came from villages and hamlets scattered far and wide and returned home only when their corn had been ground. So they stayed for several hours at the mill waiting for the miller to finish his job. Meanwhile other people would arrive with their sacks and await their turn. So people chatted, exchanging the latest gossip and news – the death of old Amélie, the damage done by the wild boar, the new priest, etc. In short, they took their time. And when it was time to pay the miller, they took a couple of rabbits out of their bag, or a plump goose, or some eels. For ready cash was not much used by the peasants of the time.

Apart from war, which obliged the miller to forsake his mill, the mills' worst enemy was fire. There was an almost permanent risk because of the flint in the grindstones and the dust from the grain. That is why mills were left wide open and the doors had no padlocks. The French expression "entrer comme dans un moulin" (to hold open house) comes about from this deliberately easy access. It has outlived its origin for there is no mill in service now either in Moulis or in Listrac. However, lovers of old mills could usefully spend some time in the northern Médoc, where several of these charming old buildings have been restored. A notable example can be in La Tour Haut Caussan, in the commune of Blaignan.

*

Together with the mills but before the vines (chronologically speaking), Moulis's other great treasure is its church. Under the Ancien Régime it was at the head of a huge diocese of several parishes in the suburbs of Bordeaux. The extent of its authority gave it a fame which reflected on the whole of the commune and, at a time when religion had more influence than it has now, Moulis was one of the Gironde's spiritual capitals. This naturally inspired people's imagination (as we shall see from its Romanesque carvings) and gave rise to several intriguing tales. "Before leaving in 1453, the English are said to have buried nine casks full of gold on the very spot where a hen landed after being thrown from the top of the church tower", Alain Viaut tells us in his excellent work *Récits et contes populaires du Bordelais*. It goes without saying that the famous casks have never

Like an old keep, the ancient windmill of Laborde bears witness to a cereal-growing past. ▶

been found but, if you feel like it, take a hen and a spade, and good luck! Another even more fanciful tale is the one about the founding of Rome. Alain Viaut tells it so well that there is no need to alter a single comma:

"One of the popes, we no longer know which, had ordered two churches to be built, one in Moulis and the other in Italy. The first place to finish the construction of its church was to be called Rome. So everyone set to work. At Moulis, stones were brought by barge from Blaye. They were unloaded at Lamarque and taken by cart as far as Moulis by the old Roman road. But the carts came late at night and from time to time one would disappear completely. People said this was the work of Léonard, Beychevelle's local wizard, who was putting a spell on them. Naturally this held the work up. But just when the church was nearly finished, two men who had just finished their dinner saw a horseman arriving. He leapt off his horse which was foaming at the mouth after the journey, and said, 'The church of Rome is finished and the Pope has already celebrated High Mass'. Everyone was dismayed. The devil had surely had a hand in this. And that is the reason why Moulis was not called Rome."

An appealing story. If Moulis had been Rome, you can be sure that the face of the world, or at least that of the Médoc, would have changed. Just imagine Chasse-Spleen as the Vatican, with trains full of pilgrims arriving at the tiny station, making a detour to Maucaillou to visit the Musée du Vin; the Pope receiving heads of state in Poujeaux's cellars or giving his *urbi et orbi* blessing from the steps of Moulin à Vent. What publicity! But it was not to be. For want of a *habemus papam*, we must be satisfied with a *habemus vinum*, which is not bad going and more than most people can say. As for the church, the exceptional quality of the genuinely Romanesque choir must be mentioned. Although no pope has said mass there, for the reasons given above, all lovers of religious art should pay it a visit. This choir is decorated with two tiers of carved and decorated blind arcading which is highly symbolic. Dogs, birds, cats and dragons intertwine in a complex and remarkable fashion. There are scallop shells, known as coquilles Saint-Jacques, reminding us of the pilgrimages to Compostella, and next to them pine cones, bunches of grapes, ears of corn, tracery and festoons, forming one of the most unusual ensembles of stone carving to be seen in the region. There is everything from the creation of the world to the struggle of Good with Evil and the ancient myths. Three influences, Norman, Saintonge and oriental, seem to have been prevalent when this stonework was carved. Certain specialists can detect precise meanings in it, such as

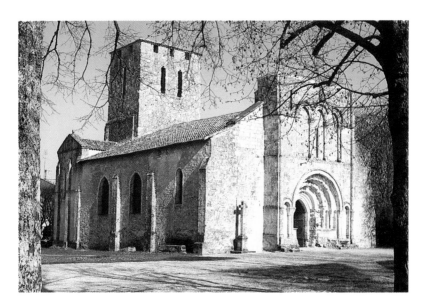

the legend of Tobias "carrying the fish whose gall was to cure his father's blindness": an interesting detail when we remember that Tobie Clarke founded the property which still bears his name a mile or so away. He was Irish, and thus a Celt, and the three arches of oak leaves symbolizing the three stages of knowledge decorating the entrance are of Celtic inspiration.

Romanesque churches are rare in the Médoc. There are about ten, which by comparison with the region of Entre-deux-Mers or Charente is not many. So the work of these twelfth-century artists in Moulis is of correspondingly greater importance. But it must be admitted that after the choir the rest of the building is less interesting. Traces of successive modifications can be seen, particularly from the seventeenth and nineteenth centuries, which certain experts do not like. But we should not forget that the mother of the famous Pey Berland, the fifteenth-century Bishop of Bordeaux, is buried here in the graveyard. Archaeologists have discovered this thanks to a stone engraved with a cross and bearing the words *"mater archipis"*. In accordance with the extensive authority of Moulis's priest, the presbytery was a large building. It is not the one used by the present-day priest, but is now in fact Château Biston, an elegant house with steep roofs, the only château in the commune which does not make wine. Today it serves as a hotel and there are very attractive "chambres d'hôte" available. This is the only evidence of modern tourism

Even more than the exterior, the choir deserves a visit. Its delightful Romanesque carvings display Norman, Saintonge and oriental influences, all impressively rich in symbolism.

in Moulis and it is entirely justified. With its discreet architecture, it fits perfectly into the surrounding countryside.

Today, it is obviously wine which is the principal activity. This is not new, but although wine already accounted for the commune's principal income in the nineteenth century, there were also other crops, grain, fodder and firewood. These were peripheral "riches" for, in 1892, out of a total area of 2,000 hectares, vines in Moulis already covered 1,500 hectares. Even more surprisingly, although there were some 9,000 plants per hectare, the commune's average yield for this vintage did not exceed 6 hectolitres per hectare. Figures a century later are revealing by comparison: in 1987 Moulis's vineyards covered 500 hectares, producing around 24,000 hectolitres of wine per year, as against 9,000 a hundred years ago. So much has changed, and not only technical and agronomic conditions, for the region's social life has also been completely transformed. At the end of the ninteenth century there were 200 vine-growing estates in Moulis, a livelihood for 800 people. Today this figure has fallen to 320 people and the number of estates has been reduced to a quarter. Fortunately, the one thing which has not diminished is the quality of the wine.

What were the effects of the River Gironde when it arrived in the inhospitable marshlands of Moulis long, long ago? Just as in Margaux and Pauillac, it deposited different-coloured stones, known in viticultural circles as gravel, brought down from the mountains in its swirling torrent. "Milky or glassy quartz, even pink, grey or blue from round Limoges, layered agates from the region of Albi, superb black lydians from the Pyrenees, black and white chert coming from the Périgord", is how René Pijassou describes them, with a geologist's precision. Without them, there would be no gravelly ridges in Moulis and probably little or no wine. For Moulis wine was born on the ridge called Grand-Poujeaux. At the close of the Middle Ages, the inhabitants already knew the virtues of this pebbly soil, thin, poor but warm and well drained, easy to work and ideal for growing vines. The first wines of Moulis were born here and the best have remained. Of the two communes of Listrac and Moulis, Grand-Poujeaux is *the* great vine-growing land, the most typical of the Médoc. It seems that its geological distinction (Gunz gravel is one of wine's best progenitors) has tended to make it proud, wanting to go it alone. So the hamlet of Grand-Poujeaux stands resolutely apart from the centre of the village, as if nature wanted it to keep its distance, being carried out with everything not without it but around it. This idea is quite in keeping with the frequently-heard statement that Grand-Poujeaux is the geographical centre of the Haut-Médoc. "The wines of Poujeaux are the best wines of Moulis," Guillon wrote in 1868 in his book *Les châteaux de la Gironde*, and he added "The newspaper *Le Producteur* reckons that they are like the wines of Saint-Julien and suggests they should be classed with the fourth *crus*, though this has not been done."

This comparison with Saint-Julien, made over a hundred years ago, is in many ways still valid today. Finding a likeness with such a prestigious appellation does not take away the personality of Moulis wines. Of course, they do not have the body or the often spectacular distinction found in certain vintages of Léoville Las-Cases or Ducru-Beaucaillou. But their roundness, mellowness and finesse are often comparable, even more so the complexity of their bouquet, and it is in this they most resemble one another. Indeed the soil and proportions of grape varieties are so similar that the opposite would have been surprising. This does not mean that Grand-Poujeaux has a monopoly as the cradle of viticulture in Moulis. The commune has other areas of Garonne gravel which are "brilliant" at Brillette, or of Pyrenean gravel at Mauvezin or Pomeys. But everywhere else, as at Listrac, it is the clayey limestone which predominates. At one time the road from Bouqueyran to Moulis was completely unusable for several months of the year because of the clay and mud. This was the reason why a chapel was built at Bouqueyran, though after being sequestered by the Revolutionary government it was completely demolished.

Now there is no more mud on the road. There are still, however, two very distinct types of land in the same appellation, which automatically implies two sorts of wines. This is why it is difficult to pinpoint precisely the individuality of Moulis wines. There are the Grand-Poujeaux and there are the others. The first are definitely like those of Margaux and Saint-Julien, and the others are nearer to a classic Listrac. But these comparisons should be qualified.

At the head of the Grand-Poujeaux, it is usual to group together Poujeaux, Chasse-Spleen and Maucaillou. And yet although they have almost the same type of soil, the difference in the wines is quite apparent. Poujeaux has more body, Chasse-Spleen more distinction and Maucaillou more charm. These differences do not affect the quality of the wine, merely their personality. And certain vintages

---

The Moulis countryside is dotted with attractive copses and woodland, as well as vineyards.

of Gressier, Dutruch or Bel-Air Lagrave can be their equal, a role sometimes also played by Brillette, Branas, Moulin à Vent, Anthonic and Biston-Brillette. "The Moulis appellation is 'in the pink'. Its name is evocative of the discreet charm which suits it so well, for it is the smallest in the Médoc," Jo Gryn aptly wrote in *Le Point*. The small appellation of Moulis, though it now produces nearly two million bottles per year, is a formidable concentration of the wine-producing Médoc. Its wine can catch out experienced tasters at blind tastings, and be mistaken either for a Graves or a Saint-Estèphe. Generally the principal variety is the cabernet-sauvignon, but there is merlot too, and certain properties have ten per cent of petit-verdot and cabernet-franc. This being so, there is no question of referring to wines of a particular variety. Moulis is individual; its wine is the very synthesis of all the possible Médocs, produced on a narrow strip of land stretching for some ten kilometres from east to west. The compensation for this relatively hemmed-in position is a finesse and harmony in the wines, which are often ideally suitable for laying down. They are wines for the gourmet, characterized by an extremely rich bouquet. They are always elegant, even in off-years.

In 1938, all these good qualities were acknowledged and officially recognized with the creation of the *appellation d'origine contrôlée* applied only to this area. This represented the end of a twenty-year struggle by the Viticultural Federation, created on January 1, 1925. Its founder was Monsieur Marly, whose *cru,* then called Poujeaux-Marly, now belongs to Château Poujeaux. After him there came successively Jean Lambert, Monsieur Goffre-Viaud, Philippe de Saint-Affrique and Jean Theil, presiding over a federation which has always been dynamic without being disruptive. Today it is François Theil, Jean's son, who has been at the helm since the death of his father. But Dominique Hessel, another Moulis grower, should also be mentioned. He is president of the powerful Conseil des Vins du Médoc (formerly the GIE), which groups together nearly all the 1,500 estates of the peninsula.

There are already several signs that the commune is beginning to be more outward-looking. A restaurant, an off-shoot of Château Clarke, has recently opened under the name of "Cercle œnologique". Provided you reserve your table in advance, you can eat marvellous steaks grilled on vine-prunings. Bee-keeping, too, should be mentioned, and you can buy all sorts of different honey produced in the hives of the Petit family. And the little *coopérative* called La Moulissoise at the crossroads at Petit-Poujeaux is relatively new but it has been a great success, selling reasonably priced good bottles from the region. Everywhere things are moving: buildings are being restored, vineyards replanted and there is a generally high level of activity. Even modern marketing techniques are being brought into play. After launching the periodical *Vinitech*, Philippe Dourthe at Maucaillou created the *Journal d'un bourgeois du Médoc*, widely distributed to his clients, sellers, friends and visitors. The Theil brothers have done the same thing at Château Poujeaux, with their *Secrets de château*, a small but attractive and well-put-together pamphlet serving to make the finer details of their wines better known. And lastly, in 1987 at Château Brillette, Monique Berthault, who is never short of ideas, launched the unusual *Cuvée du millénaire*, dedicated to Hugues Capet, with his portrait on the front label and the royal monogram on the back. This is how the 75 vintage of Brillette will go down in history, thanks to this publicity, very much in line with modern tastes. It is true that in recent years Moulis has been keen to extend its facilities for welcoming visitors, and wine is the principal reason for this. Its fame is spreading and rightly, for it reflects the progress noted in the quality of its wines. An increasing part of the annual production goes for export, Belgium being the principal importer, followed by Switzerland and Holland. This is positive proof that the appellation is appreciated, for the Walloons, Flemish and Swiss have long been recognized as wine connoisseurs.

In these conditions, the little village of mills can look confidently to the future. With its old legends, its large pebbles gleaming in the sun and its delicious wines, Moulis does honour to all the vineyards of Bordeaux. Recently, attractive signs have sprung up on the roadsides announcing that Moulis is "the appellation in the heart of the Médoc". This is quite true, and we could even add that if Moulis is the heart of the Médoc, it is also the Médoc closest to our hearts.

A force of nature

"Listrac has at least two good leagues of land stretching from east to west and one league from north to south, and so covers a considerable area in all. At Listrac there are different types of land, some stony, some gravelly, others of heavy soil, and there is a considerable expanse of meadowland," wrote the priest Baurein in 1781. "It is a big village with a splendid church and, of all the communes along the river, this is the one which has most meadows," wrote Charles Cocks in 1850. "The principal income of this commune comes from wine, cereal crops and firewood. On the west, there is a huge area of meadowland, enabling the farmers to breed sheep," wrote Pierre Hugon in 1855. Putting these different descriptions together, we can glean a good idea of the true nature of Listrac and of what it looks like today. The people of Listrac were born at the foot of the vines but they grew up alongside the cattle, as they readily admit in this commune whose three principal activities are vine-growing, cattle farming and forestry. To unearth its history is to go right back to the traces of a Celtic settlement whose remains were found at Peyrelebade and Le Mayne-de-Lalande. Later, the widespread parish of Listrac, consisting of several hamlets often at a considerable distance from one another, was dependent on the powerful barony of Vertheuil. In the fifteenth century it belonged to Bernard of Lesparre, becoming part of the seigniory of Castelnau, its close neighbour. The existence of several noble houses and the traditional role of the local monks ensured the cultivation of vines from the end of the Middle Ages. And the road running right through the centre of the village made it easier to sell the wine. But the inhabitants had other rural activities. Firstly

◄ *Saint Catherine of Alexandria is one of Listrac's patronsaints.*

At an altitude of 43 metres, Listrac is the highest point in the vine-growing Médoc. ►

there was cattle and sheep breeding, followed by cereal crops. For unlike land made up simply of gravelly soil, outstanding for wine but almost useless for anything else, the soil of Listrac, which has more clay and so is more fertile, made it possible to grow traditional crops. The ruins of a number of mills are evidence of this. In the nineteenth century widespread planting of pine trees took place in what has now become forest on the west of the commune. The result is that today there are some 4,500 hectares of pine trees belonging in the main to small proprietors. Business in resin has dropped off considerably by comparison with the first half of the century, but the

forest is still one of the region's considerable riches. There are many growers who are also foresters.

The proximity of the forest is important, too, for it is said to have an effect on the wine's flavour. Some say that the west wind gives the grapes a scent of resin. When the wine is in the glass, it has an aroma at once sweet and spicy, that perfume so characteristic of pine trees at the end of summer. So Listrac wine has another side to its personality, redolent of resin and the forests. This should be taken with a pinch of salt. At the risk of spoiling the charm of such legends, it should be said that no serious analysis has ever supported this suggestion. I think that people who have been fortunate enough to find a breath of the forest in their glasses have forgotten to mention that their dining-room window, looking out on a large forest of pine trees, was open that day.

Listrac is more remarkable for its geography than for its history. The origin of its apparently Roman name goes back to the low Latin word *lista*, meaning boundary. It is the limit of the two Médocs, that of the estuary to the east and that of the forests to the west – of the "Ribeyrons" (the river men) and of the "Landescots" (foresters) as the old Médoc dialect called the inhabitants of the peninsula, according to whether they lived by the river or not. This semi-frontier position comes about from its "altitude", for in relation to the surrounding plain, Listrac is like a crest, a dividing line between the river and the sea. The highest vineyard in all the Médoc is that of Fonréaud at the entrance to the village where there is the fire watchtower, forty-three metres above sea level. But the actual highest point in Listrac is the hamlet of Berniquet, which proudly claims forty-four metres. Jules-Irénée Meyre, who is nearing 80 and has a prodigious memory, remembers living in Berniquet in his childhood. He recalls that on the same farm, water drained away in two different directions: the water from the well and the domestic pump ran away towards the stream in Fonréaud and so eventually reached the Garonne; the other, the water used in the cattle-shed, went to the forest canals, and so to the lake at Carcans. So there were two slopes falling away opposite each other, at some fifty metres distance. You might well think you were in the mountains.

In a way, Listrac also looks rather like a mountain village. Old houses (some of them charming) stand on the narrow, sloping roads around the church. This is an extremely old building whose pointed rustic belfry has been built onto Romanesque remains. It is considered less important than that of Moulis (and rightly so), but this is a lively parish nevertheless. The great religious festivals are celebrated to the accompaniment of a very good choir and the village's long-established music society, a small amateur orchestra whose brass instruments resound at the end of mass in a generally well-attended church.

And what could be more natural than to drink Listrac wine at mass? For wine has been known here at least since the fifteenth century. The first text which refers to it dates from 1470, giving a family of serfs their freedom, for which they had to provide a *tonneau* of wine (in casks) and a pair of hens every Michaelmas, as the excellent local historian Alain Viaut tells us. The same thing

happened in 1536 when another charter of emancipation mentions casks of wine in exchange for freedom. Clearly the feudal system already considered wine as a form of wealth. The system has long disappeared, but in view of the development of modern viticulture we might be tempted to think that in this respect it was rather forward-looking.

"Listrac was the only wine sufficiently sturdy to withstand the constant vibration of the trains without losing any of its qualities. I remember I was always amazed by this... Dear Listrac wine, so unmistakeably a force of nature!" This is what the scholarly Jean Dutourd of the *Académie française* wrote in a humorous text composed for a publicity pamphlet about Château Clarke and published by the magazine *Médoc*, the mouthpiece of the Conseil des Vins du Médoc. The link between Listrac wines and the railways is given full coverage elsewhere (see Grand Listrac), but I cannot resist quoting Jean Dutourd once more, if only to pay tribute to his love of the good wines of Listrac:

▲ *Listrac's lovely little church, ready to welcome faithful shepherds, foresters and vignerons.*

"I always associate this Bordeaux wine with the attractive decor of the dining-cars on excursion trains. There was loin of veal and *endives au gratin,* served on tables covered with elegant white table-cloths and battered silver. The chairs had Louis XV feet. You passed the salt-cellar to a young woman, all alone, pretending to read a Cronin novel. Who would not sing the praises of those dining-cars, as sumptuous as the Second Empire hotels in the Parc Monceau? Who could describe the queues of starving travellers waiting for the whistle for second service? Who would not swear to the delicious and romantic nature of the Company's execrable menu?

"We would always order a half-bottle of Listrac (it only came in half-bottles, a mystery I have never been able to solve). It had various qualities. Firstly, it was very good, and a real Bordeaux. Secondly, it was the cheapest on the wine list. And lastly it was to be found only here, leading us to suppose that the SNCF had bought up all the wine that was produced.

"The dining-cars have disappeared. They have been replaced by the dreary self-service counters which have so wonderfully succeeded in serving even worse food accompanied by an anonymous plonk or those pitiful fruit juices which are supposed to have reduced the level of alcoholism in France. Alas! The Listrac disappeared with the dining-cars. A whole civilization swallowed up!"

But no, it has not vanished. "The Listrac has reappeared, even more full-bodied, more charming, better than before," Jean Dutourd concludes, a sign that the epic days of the dining-cars have given way to a new era. "More full-bodied", he says. And the news is out. Listrac wines have a body, power and virility which make the appellation the most consistent in the Médoc. However old the bottle you open may be, the wine always seems young. I will always remember the amazement of two ancient growers for whom I had opened an old bottle of Listrac. They found it delicious (and so it was), but when I asked them to tell me its approximate vintage, they placed it between 1964 and 1970. In fact it was a Saransot-Dupré 1924, of unbelievable freshness and with a splendid harmony in its bouquet. It was perfect, except that after careful analysis, its finish suggested it was perhaps just a bit too young.

This unwillingness to age, this suitability for long keeping, is its hallmark, and typical of Listrac. Even its colour resists the passing years. In time, the majority of Médocs change from ruby to brick-red. Listracs change from garnet-red to ruby! You really have to come across a poor year to find an orange tint. Furthermore, with these vintages, "when the Médocs are thin, the wines of Listrac are

Un côté du vignoble SARANSOT-DUPRÉ (Listrac-Médoc).

often recognized as among the best," considers Féret, so paying homage to their consistency. The wine's solid structure derives quite naturally from the land which produces it. For a long time this land was one huge cornfield, when it was not left fallow for pasture. We might well wonder if over the centuries the straw and manure together have not made it especially fertile. This secret alchemy has not been proved by modern science, but it is amusing to sniff out its beneficial effects. But this is not to detract from the virtues of the soil itself, whose base of clayey limestone promotes fertility.

Full-bodied, virile and solid, the wine of Listrac owes its robust constitution partly to the methods of the people who make it. The land gives them a robust product but, more so than other growers in the Médoc, the men of Listrac have long worked in the old way. They have not tried to make their wines more supple and, in a word, more marketable. Of all the Médoc appellations, it is the most natural wine, vinified so that its naturally rich constituent elements should keep well in the bottle. Tasters have often found Listracs hard, closed up, austere and sometimes even rustic. But these are the very qualities of a little wine from a small grower, with its charms and its risks. Even today, small producers keep their wine in very old casks for three years or more and expect to bottle it only when they have time. Young growers laugh at this, but their grandfathers before them never did otherwise. It was said then that a good vintage could be drunk after ten years and a great one after twenty, with the implication that during these twenty years the wine was not good.

▲ *Sixty years ago, mechanization of the vineyards helped to increase the size of the parcels.*

Of all the Médocs, Listrac is the wine which the merchants have left most on the fringe. Because the cooperative had direct business with the railways, the merchants cold-shouldered – and still do in a way – an appellation they wanted to punish for not having worked with them. At the time when the merchants were the only agents for Bordeaux wines, particularly abroad, Listrac did not jump on the export wagon; it was being drunk in other wagons! As a result, the producers have remained rather out on a limb, even isolated, and unlike the rest have not benefited from the often prudent advice merchants can give their suppliers. This mentality is gradually changing but only slowly. The market imposes on the producer the need for a wine which is rounder, livelier and more open, and which can be drunk younger. Oenology helps him to achieve this without being unfaithful to his product, which often still remains "a force of nature". We no longer have to wait twenty years to uncork a bottle. Ten will do.

There were two Rothschilds in Pauillac; in Listrac there is a third. When Baron Edmond came to chateau Clarke in 1973, the news spread far and wide. The estate was uncultivated and the château in ruins. Everyone said "he's mad" or rather nearly everyone, for a few of the more astute Listrac people realized at once that to have a Rothschild in the appellation was going to give it an almighty boost. Obviously when he replanted Clarke, and then some years later the neighbouring estate of Peyrelebade, the Baron aroused a legitimate curiosity which reflected on all the other producers. There had never been so much talk about Listrac: magazines had page upon page of photographs of the stretches of vineyards restored around a newly created château. The ever-smiling Baroness, Nadine, took part in the publicity with that natural charm for which she is so well known. The enormous amount of work carried out over one hundred and fifty hectares has shouted to the world that a Rothschild, one of the greatest fortunes in France, has invested in Listrac. Obviously that is bound to have side-effects. Although we should keep things in proportion, the arrival of the football player Jean Tigana in the spring of 1987 was yet one more vote of confidence for the people of Listrac. After Rothschild, Tigana! It was almost too good to be true. An outstanding sportsman, probably one of the best of his generation in the world, Jean Tigana was already virtually a neighbour. For

---

Jean, Yves and Jean-François Gobinaud, descended from a very old Listrac family, at work in their vat-house. ▶

since he has played for the team of the Girondins, he has more or less belonged to Bordeaux. One fine day, he arrived in Listrac to visit Château Pierre Bibian, and he bought it. For a football player to turn grower was a new feather in the commune's cap – and what prestige for the appellation!

So, thanks to wine, Listrac has its stars. The fact has not radically changed the village. It remains as it always has been, basically agricultural, genuine and welcoming. The proof of this was seen at the beginning of the sixties, when several French families, such as the Chanfreaus, the Pagès and the Thérons, returned from Algeria to settle here. Growers in North Africa, they slipped easily into the rhythm of things here and today some of them are the best ambassadors for the land they have adopted. There are no "outsiders" in Listrac; everybody makes wine together. It is as simple as that. But you must understand that they do not all make the same wine, for in that case one single label would be enough for the hundred and four producers in the appellation. As we have seen, Listrac wines have a family likeness but they are different, depending on their terrain and their vintner. The commune is so widespread that each hamlet retains its own personality. On the gravelly land of Couhenne, where, aptly enough, Château Belgrave is to be found, there is a natural resemblance to the nearby ridges of Cussac. Those of Médrac, twins of those in Grand-Poujeaux, produce a wine very like those of Moulis. And the terrain of Donissan or Marcieux is not the same as that of Le Fourcas or Laborde. The goat grazes where it is tethered, as they used to say in the country. The same is true of vines, which adapt themselves to their soil.

Every bit of land here has its own history. The little area of Lafon alone merits a chapter to itself. Before the war, a grower called Camille Bernard lived at Lafon. He too was a force of nature. When the oxen drew the convoys of carts full of casks to the port of Lamarque, where they were loaded onto barges for the boatmen to take down to the merchants on the Quai des Chartrons in Bordeaux, Camille Bernard was always there to travel with them. For he was the only man in the region capable of lifting the casks. And full ones at that! With 125 litres of wine in them, without counting the weight of the wood, each weighed something like 250 kilos, or five hundredweight, which our hero lifted with ease. One day, egged on by his friends, he bet that he could overturn a cartload of manure all by himself. Nobody believed him, until he took two of the wheel's wooden spokes firmly in his hands and gently lifted it into the air.

He won his bet.

Also at Lafon, one fine day during the nineteenth century, there arrived a soldier from the routed Spanish army in flight. His name was Arcansole, or at least that is what they called him. Unaided, he built his house, made a sundial which he fixed over the front door and, again without any help, cleared several hectares of meadow in order to plant vines. Then his son-in-law came to Lafon and started a wine merchant's warehouse. But business was bad and he went bust. He was declared bankrupt and one morning the bailiffs came to impound his wine. They seized all the casks and took them to the square in Castelnau to auction them. It was then that they saw that they were not filled with wine, but water! Everybody was highly amused except the men from the revenue. Somehow or other, the merchant had been tipped off and during the night had removed his wine. Where to? No one knows, for it was never seen again.

Such are the stories that used to be handed down by word of mouth by old folk to their grandchildren. While making clogs out of alder wood or a yoke from heart of elm, they handed down the village's irreplaceable heritage. That is why Listrac, an old, solid and smiling region, seems so engaging. As for the wine, this definition by oenologist Jacques Boissenot is all that is required. There is no one better qualified to describe it:

"The wine of Listrac is extraordinarily big full and lasting on the palate. When they taste it, wine lovers find it a wine to be chewed, for its texture is so tight. Solidly constructed, with much tannin, well structured, it is the perfect marriage of the fruit of the cabernet and the power of the merlot. This makes it full, smooth, lively and virile."

The development of rail and road transport has gradually caused the disappearance of river traffic. Here a faithful old Berliet wagon is loaded with barriques at Château Saransot-Dupré.

A painter in light

Odilon Redon was born in Bordeaux on April 20, 1840, near the allées Damour, which after the war became the place des Martyrs de la Résistance. It is a square dominated by the elegant church of Saint-Seurin, where the painter first took communion. A mere biographical detail, you may say. Not a bit of it: for it was here during the ceremony that the painter says he felt " a great emotion" and that "art first spoke" to him through the canticles he heard. And yet, if we were to dig still deeper in search of the roots of his inspiration, we should have to go to Listrac, to the estate of Peyrelebade where Redon spent part of his early life.

"In this old manor I was looked after first by a nurse and then by an old uncle, the estate manager, whose kind features and blue eyes are one of my strongest childhood memories." Thus wrote Redon in the diary he kept for nearly fifty years, later published by the Librairie José Corti under the title *A soi-même* ("To Himself"). This book is important for the deeper understanding it provides of the influence of the Médoc on the artist, of which there is much evidence in his works.

Peyrelebade is at the top of a chalky knoll, and from the house there are uninterrupted views through 360 degrees over immense stretches of vineyards, moors, meadows and forests. Silence, nature and clouds all exercised a sort of fascination over the artist. But he was especially intrigued, it would seem, by the light and the trees. With its elevated position, Listrac enjoys an exceptional light, often enhanced by troubled skies. He seems also to have fallen under the spell of this timeless region, given over to forests on one side and crops on the other, captivated by its wealth of arcane legends and its rural melancholy. If Redon was a romantic before becoming a symbolist, Peyrelebade was one of the prime causes. "It is to my region that I owe these sad faces you see. I have drawn them because I have seen them and because the eyes of childhood have preserved

them clearly in my inmost soul. Yes, an ancient wall, an old tree, a distant horizon can inspire the artist and provide him with all his essential needs. The day Rembrandt advised his pupils against travelling, especially to Italy, I believe he was the speakin as the herald of true art."

This old tree, that ancient wall, Redon has reproduced them ten times, a hundred times over in his paintings; trees with black trunks and often skeletal branches, and vast skies, frequently seeming to overpower the land. In his more vividly coloured paintings, whether of the pool, the road or the house at Peyrelebade, everything is drowned in the shade of the trees. And before moving off into a world of unreality, the work of Redon begins here at Listrac, with *Charrettes cassées* or *Chevaux au pâturage*, reflections of the rural

▲ *Odilon Redon's "Le Chemin de Peyrelebade", with the dominant blue tones so characteristic of his work.*

life among which he spent his childhood. Strangely, there are no vines. Would they have implied a landscape in which man's influence was too strong? Or was it because the precise alignment of the vine rows conflicted with the artist's sense of inner turmoil? We do not know and he himself gives us no explanation. But there is not one single bunch of grapes in his works, in which nature has such an important place! We can only suppose that he deliberately rejected the familiar sight of the vines and the harvests, preferring to take refuge in secret dreams and reveries.

In the Médoc Redon also discovered Soulac and the Atlantic. "Painters, go and look at the sea. You will see wonderful effects of colour and light and a glittering sky. You will feel the poetry of the sand, the charm of the air and infinite subtleties. You will return with new strength and full of song." This exhortation, almost a confession, clearly reveals his state of mind, as do his drawings of the dunes. The movement of the water, the sand, the clouds or the pines "creating a continual murmuring sadness" drew the artist into deep meditation as he communed with his inner self. But for him Peyrelebade was also a place of tragedy, for his first son, Jean, died there in 1886, when he was only a few months old. "Peyrelebade was just a hamlet, so to speak, and he had captivated the place. People were always stopping me to ask, 'Is he asleep? How is he?' Children would say: 'Where is your little boy?'... Jean was always delighted by greenery, and on the rare occasions when he cried if we put him under the chestnut tree in the garden he would soon stop." His di-

▲ *A Listrac sketch by Redon.*

"L'Automne en Médoc": an example of the fascination that the light of this region held for the painter.

▶

ary has three wonderful pages about the birth and death of this first child. What is written, with touching reserve, barely conceals what is hidden between the lines.

In 1897 there came a bolt from the blue: the house at Peyrelebade was sold. Family arguments and disputes over inheritance came to disrupt this simple, peaceful spot. For Odilon Redon it was a blow from which he was to suffer until his death in 1916, and which he summed up in these words: "I feel as if all my roots have been torn up." The intimate link, which for fifty-seven years had bound him to his childhood, to his family and to nature, was broken. His art was to bear the scars, though from then on Redon gradually abandoned sombre tones and charcoal sketches and turned to the bright colours which mingle with some exuberance in his later canvases. Even though deprived of his property, or perhaps because of it, Redon continued to draw singular inspiration from it. He was filled with Listrac's magic throughout his life, which ended in Paris on July 6, 1916. He was 76, and less anxious for himself than for his son Arï, fighting on the front in the terrible battles of the First World War. Arï Redon and his wife Suzanne bequeathed the art collection they had inherited from the painter to the state: a hundred and sixty sketches and pastel drawings and eighty oil paintings. Today many are exhibited in the musée d'Orsay in Paris, notably the *Maison de Peyrelebade*, hidden among the trees in bright summer sunlight. The musée des beaux arts in Bordeaux also has some of Redon's works, in particular views of the meadows and forests of the Médoc.

In the eighteenth century Peyrelebade had been one of the largest vine-growing estates of Listrac, with one thousand five hundred *journaux* of vines (a *journal,* equivalent to the English acre, was the area of land which a man could work in one day). From the beginning of the nineteenth century, the vineyard declined to one hundred and twenty *journaux,* and five proprietors succeeded one another in a short space of time: Monsieur Testas, Madame Olanyer, Maître Darrieu (a notary from Bordeaux), Monsieur Cluzet and Monsieur Lacaze. Odilon Redon's father acquired the estate in 1835 on his return from a series of long voyages, and the Redons held it for sixty-two years. Strangely enough, Charles Cocks does not mention Peyrelebade among the *crus* of Listrac in his first edition of *Bordeaux et ses vins* in 1850, although he lists sixty different growers in the commune. We shall see in the catalogue how this estate has now regained its position under the recent impetus given it by Baron Edmond de Rothschild.

Odilon Redon was a highly individual artist whose life overlapped not only two centuries but also two worlds: one of outward realities and the other of inner torments. Would he have been the same if he had not found in Listrac, and throughout the Médoc, so many of the elements which influenced his art? Probably not. "We are tied to certain places by invisible bonds which give man's creativity life," he wrote about the old house at Peyrelebade. 1990 marked the 150th anniversary of the birth of Odilon Redon. Not a single celebration commemorated this occasion. This year simply represented the accomplishment of the estate's period of renaissance and the establishment of a steady cruising speed; after a few initial difficulties, the estate is now on a sound footing. None the less, the memory of the painter still lives here. The horses are gone, the elms have been cut down, the brambles have disappeared, but the pool he painted is still there, and with it there remains the memory of Odilon Redon, born to paint the changing skies of Listrac.

"Allez les petits!"

Statistics are tedious but from time to time they are useful, on condition that they are viewed like an instant photograph, to be compared with others to impart some sort of "relativity" to any final analysis. In round terms, Moulis and Listrac represent 100 families of professional growers and 1,000 hectares of vines, that is one per cent of all the vineyards in Gironde, taking all the appellations into account, including table wine. One per cent is not much. But for prestige, quality and age, the percentage is of a different order. Here are a few more figures: over the last ten years, more than 200 hectares of additional vines have been planted in the two appellations. And in six years, from the 1982-1983 season to that of 1987-1988, the volume marketed rose from 24,000 hectolitres to 42,000 hectolitres, a substantial increase and a praiseworthy effort by the producers, who often are also the distributors of their own wine. More figures: the home market absorbed 28,000 of the 42,000 hectolitres, that is nearly two-thirds. This is something new for the communal appellations of the Médoc, which traditionally sell the majority of their wines abroad. It is interesting to know who is drinking these wines and where they are to be found. According to a recent survey conducted by the Conseil Interprofessionnel des Vins de Bordeaux, the middle class accounts for 60% of what is commonly called family consumption, the upper middle class representing only 15%. Geographically speaking, the place of honour is held by the Paris region, the north and the east, since these three regions account for 40% of the market. As for retail outlets, these have changed slightly. The region producing the wine accounted for 21% of sales in 1981; nowadays, it represents only 15%. At the same time, hypermarkets and supermarkets have increased their sales from 43% to 60%. And sales by specialist wine merchants (16% of the total in 1981) have fallen by half. It is clear that chain stores are increasing their hold on the market. There are producers who are unaware of this, indeed some

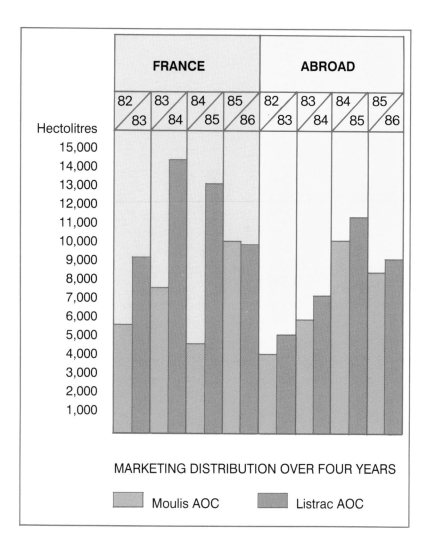

	FRANCE				**ABROAD**			
Hectolitres	82/83	83/84	84/85	85/86	82/83	83/84	84/85	85/86

MARKETING DISTRIBUTION OVER FOUR YEARS

Moulis AOC   Listrac AOC

who even make it their duty not to know, with the completely outdated excuse that the place for a great wine is not on the shelves of a supermarket. What a depressing mistake! Instead of surrounding themselves with a cloak of nostalgic memories of wines sent off to the Russian Court, it would be better to update the labels to try to tempt shoppers as they pass by with their trolleys.

In the export field Belgium is far and away the best customer for Moulis wines, followed by Switzerland which has increased its imports of Listrac wines tenfold over the last ten years. Next come Holland, Denmark, Great Britain and West Germany. The United States is a case apart. In 1984-1985 it bought a record quantity of 5,000 hectolitres of Moulis and Listrac, for the first time ever! It was too good to last and the following year there was a new record, the

lowest, for America imported only 1,000 hectolitres. However, the United States imported only 450 hectolitres of Moulis and Listrac in 1979-1980, while our dear Belgian friends were bravely buying 2,400 hectolitres. But wine has many friends all over the world. In 1985, according to official customs records, one hundred and fifty-six countries imported wine from Bordeaux. The United Kingdom was the largest purchaser, with 250,000 hectolitres, costing 620 million francs. The smallest was Kuwait, which spent a mere 3,000 francs – perhaps for a single old magnum of Yquem? And finally we should note the indisputable efforts of Botswana (26 hectolitres), the Virgin Islands (638 hectolitres) and Honduras (49 hectolitres). But not a single bottle to Mongolia or Uganda! An economic deputation should be sent urgently with a few samples.

▲ *When the wine was dispatched in casks, the* cru's *name would be branded on one end of the cask (Collection Château Anthonic).*

The final figures concern the yields: but let us not rush into things. I can already hear the eternal critics accusing the producers of pushing the yields too high, with a detrimental effect on quality. They should know that in 1985, because of frost in January, the Moulis appellation harvested an average of 35 hectolitres per hectare, half as much as certain other appellations at least as well known. They should also know that in 1984, because of faulty pollination of the merlots, the Listrac appellation harvested an average of 26 hectolitres per hectare, half the usual amount. The following year, again on account of the cold, these same Listracs did not exceed 43 hectolitres per hectare, whereas the figure at Saint-Estèphe was 63, which is still not excessive. As for prices, without the spectacular two hundred per cent increase noted in Saint-Julien over five years, Moulis and Listrac wines have benefited from a definite price rise. Roughly speaking the cost per *tonneau* rose from 10,000 francs at the end of 1981 to 15,000 in June 1990. But this is the price for sales in bulk, and apart from the cooperative this is not common practice in our two villages, where producers are increasingly bottling at the château and selling only by the bottle. So it will be of more use to the wine lover to know that he can find excellent bottles at Moulis and Listrac costing less than fifty francs and even less than thirty, and to know that they will age without any problem providing his cellar is protected from temperature changes, undesirable vibrations, bad smells and... burglars.

One thousand hectares and one hundred families is thus the total for the two smallest appellations in the Médoc. They would even be the smallest of all the Bordeaux AOCs if Canon-Fronsac (300 hectares), Côtes de France and Graves de Vayres (approximately 250 hectares) were not even tinier. This diminutiveness is why the Listrac appellation was granted after the others and could even have prevented Moulis from ever having an independent communal appellation. In other words they both nearly remained anonymous, which today would have detracted from their unmistakably individual personalities. But even if the vineyards of Moulis represent only a thin strip of land in the heart of the Haut-Médoc, it is right that their wines should have their own name. Overlooked by the official classifications, despite the outcries and protests which this omission provoked, they received a modest but justified compensation when

The cave, *"La Moulissoise", always extends a warm welcome to visitors, who can find*
a good cross-section of the appellation's wines there. ▶

they became independent appellations in their own right in 1938. As regards Listrac, it was unquestionably the fame resulting from its links with the wagons-lits which convinced the authorities to make an effort on behalf of the growers and recognize their public service, so to speak. There were two decrees, one for Moulis, dated May 14, 1938, and the other for Listrac, dated June 8, 1957, stipulating that the wines with the right to the *appellation contrôlée* must come from cabernet-sauvignon, cabernet-franc, carmenère, merlot and petit-verdot varieties and from no others, especially hybrids, of which there was a great number at the time. "Young vines cannot be counted as part of the total size until after the fourth year", the text adds and goes on: "The only approved system of pruning is by rods and buds, the future wood being pruned down to one eye." In other words, every precaution had been taken to make the ruling as precise as possible. So Moulis and Listrac became members of the great AOCs' club, a closed shop at whose door many vine-growing regions of the Gironde are knocking today, particularly in the Médoc and Graves. Apart from the very recently created Pessac-Léognan appellation, it seems that the door in question does not open at the drop of a hat. At a certain moment, there was even talk of making Moulis and Listrac into one single appellation, which would have been highly prejudicial to the local producers of course.

In fact, because Moulis harvests on land in Listrac and wine coming from Moulis may sometimes have a Listrac label, the INAO (Institut National des Appellations d'Origine) had to give the question serious consideration. This complicated situation had to be put into some sort of order, for it clearly did not conform with the rules. So the idea sprang up of linking Moulis and Listrac together and creating the appellation Moulis-Listrac, in the style of Barsac-Sauternes, which cleverly linked their destiny without losing their individuality. The matter caused quite a stir in Moulis and Listrac. Jokers suggested joining head and tail, calling the new appellation "Moulistrac". "No," said others, "you must take the first syllable of Moulis and the first of Listrac to give MOU-LIS, so joining the two!" "That will not do," replied a third group. "You should take the second syllable of Moulis and the second syllable of Listrac and christen the infant LIS-TRAC." This lighthearted game had the merit of being amusing but, curiously enough, did not make any of the experts at the Land Registry Office laugh. Moulis or Listrac. Was a choice really necessary? Some growers were in favour of a union with their neighbour and a change of name. But they were in the minority, as most of the producers wanted to preserve their appellation (and still do). Their reasons are quite understandable, for it is not after a thirty or fifty years'struggle to promote a name which is just beginning to become well known that it should be changed. There are more than fifty different appellations in Gironde. Will one more or one less improve the profession or make the laws more respected?

These arguments won the day. There is no longer any question of joining Moulis and Listrac together, at least for the moment. Good sense prevailed over red tape. Even so, the law must have the last say, for the law is the law. A new decree is to be issued to clarify matters,

putting an end to laxity on one hand and making things conform

with reality on the other. Estates straddling the two communes must choose, either one or the other: they cannot have their cake and eat it! In other words, parcels yielding Moulis wine will be classed as Moulis and likewise for Listrac. Thus new communal boundaries will be fixed, causing revisions that are troublesome perhaps, but nevertheless necessary so that everybody knows where they stand.

I am inclined to think that this solution is the least painful of all. For a change of appellation should be based on serious considerations, notably geographical or historical ones. If it is the terrain which is responsible for everything, as so many growers are pleased

▲ *Also at Listrac, the Maison du Vin sells local wines in a simple and friendly atmosphere.*

to tell us, Grand-Poujeaux would deserve an appellation of its own. And should we then add the magnificent gravelly land of Arcins and Lamarque, its nearest neighbours, to make a consistent geological unity, in other words, robbing Peter to pay Paul - taking away the best of Moulis and creating an even smaller appellation? Certainly not, for there is no doubt that the legislature has got it more or less right. It failed to foresee certain unexpected excesses which must be corrected today, but there is little point in dwelling on that. It is not the name which makes the wine better; it is the soil, the sun and the people. And the people of the Médoc are content with their lot: "My glass is not large but I drink from my glass," as they say.

Furthermore, whether bound by a common name or "living in sin", Moulis and Listrac would not necessarily be any better off. It is not only their wines but their village life, their hamlets, their reassuring, authentic traditions and their supposed smallness (although they are known worldwide), which make them highly appreciated today. We can always dream of motorways, intersections, flashy advertisements, and so on. But I think that when there are no more flowers on the roadside, the wine will no longer taste the same. Here

---

▲ *The newcomer Jean Tigana, football star and proprietor of Pierre Bibian, shown here with Michel Lescoutra, mayor of Listrac, and Maurice Meyre, president of the* cave coopérative *of Grand Listrac.*

◄ *The Hôtel de France in Listrac serves traditional regional cuisine. Château Clarke can accomodate groups and prides training courses in tasting.*

civilization has called a halt wherever it risked disturbing nature, and if it has disturbed it, at least it has repaired the damage. More than anywhere else these precautions help to create a keen awareness of humanity, and respect for the land, acquired long ago, would seem to be the reason. Moulis and Listrac produce wine and something more, because they are not huge machines geared to an intensive marketing, because they do not imitate the "greats" though secretly they come very close to them, because they create feelings and not sensations, and because they have firmly made their mark and their future is ensured. I invite you now to come and visit each grower, one by one - but to take full advantage of the visit, be sure to have a glass in your hand.

*Drawing of a vine-leaf
by Odilon Redon.*

Catalogue
of crus

In order to know whether a *cru* has the Moulis or the Listrac appellation, the reader should refer to the wine's commune, indicated in the data at the beginning of each entry.

The number of coloured glasses beside a *cru* gives an idea of value for money it represents. This estimation, while arrived at as objectively as possible, is naturally subject to discussion and to change. It is intended as a rough guide and has no official standing as a classification.

Certain châteaux have one or more different labels for other wines produced by the property (for example wines from young vines). Such wines are followed by an arrow which indicates the château of origin.

This symbol indicates that a particular name is the secondary wine of a larger estate.

The quantities given for wine produced indicate a general average.

CB This denotes château-bottled.

Anthonic (Château)

Cru bourgeois supérieur

Commune: Moulis-en-Médoc. **Proprietor:** Pierre Cordonnier. Vineyard manager: Pierre Garbay. Consultant oenologist: Jacques Boissenot, Lamarque. **Size of vineyard:** 16 hectares. **Average age of vines:** 12 years. **Varieties:** 65% cabernet-sauvignon, 30% merlot, 5% petit-verdot. **Production:** 85 *tonneaux,* 100,000 bottles CB. **Visits:** François Cordonnier, tel. 56 58 02 55. **Marketing:** 70% for export and 30% sold to the trade and private clients.

Originally, in the nineteenth century, this château was called Puy-de-Menjon; it became Graves Queytignan at the beginning of the twentieth century and today it is Château Anthonic. There are very few estates which have changed their name three times in a hundred years in a region where loyalty to the past sometimes takes on religious proportions. Classed as a *bourgeois supérieur* in 1932, Anthonic belonged for a long time to the Hugon family, one of the oldest in the area. But troubles came one after the other – economic crisis, the war, frost – and reduced it to a pitiful state. In 1977, Pierre Cordonnier undertook the restoration of the vineyard and the business, and today we see his successful results: 16 hectares of vines under production bondering Château Clarke in a soil of clayey limestone, typical of the north side of the Moulis appellation. The cellars and vat-house have also been restored. Thirty per cent of the casks are renewed every year and the wine is vinified in stainless steel vats equipped with temperature control. Rather tannic and hard when young, because of the vines' youth, the wine is certain to age well and is now regaining its former position. Seventy per cent goes for export. In this, Pierre Cordonnier can be relied on to ensure excellent marketing of his wine. For apart from being a grower and vintner in Moulis, he is a wine-broker in Brussels where, among others, he represents the firm of J.P. Moueix, the well-known merchants in

Pierre Garbay, the vineyard manager at Anthonic and Dutruch Grand Poujeaux.

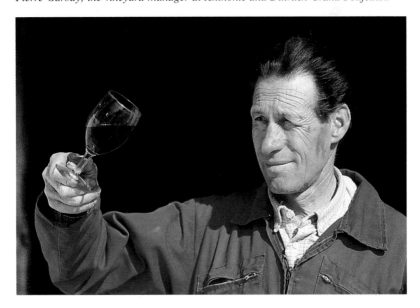

Château Anthonic sits happily in the flat landscape of the Médoc.

Libourne and joint owners of the famous Château Pétrus in Pomerol. Moreover, Pierre Cordonnier is the brother and neighbour of François, the owner of Dutruch-Grand-Poujeaux. So in the absence of Pierre, François comes along to see that all is well at Anthonic and in exchange, Pierre sells his brother's excellent wine in Belgium. In short, there is a working family arrangement. The Cordonniers in Moulis are a likeable family from the north, and their wines do them credit. Dutruch is one of the appellation's classics and Anthonic is in the process of becoming one too. It reappeared in its present form only from the 81 vintage which, like the 82, is rather marked by the vines' youth. The 83 already has much more charm and the 85s and 86s are clearly among the best. This is all very promising. It will be interesting to watch Anthonic's progress closely as it gradually becomes one of the great wines of Moulis.

There is a story about the label with its picture of two eagles, one bringing the other down as they fight viciously over a bunch of grapes. Formerly, in difficult times when the wine did not sell well or sold for next to nothing, the local growers

considered this drawing as a symbol (and an apt one) of the merchant crushing the producer. This interpretation no longer holds good today. Or hardly.

Bel-Air Lagrave (Château)

Commune: Moulis-en-Médoc. **Proprietor:** Jeanne Bacquey. Consultant oenologist: C.E.I.O. Pauillac (M. Couasnon). **Size of vineyard:** 9 hectares. **Average age of vines:** 30 years. **Varieties:** 60% cabernet-sauvignon, 35% merlot, 5% petit-verdot. **Production:** 40 *tonneaux,* 45,000 bottles CB. **Visits:** weekdays from 9 a.m. to noon and 2 to 7 p.m. **Direct sales and by mail order:** in France and abroad. Jeanne Bacquey, Grand-Poujeaux, Moulis-en-Médoc, 33480 Castelnau-de-Médoc. Tel. 56 58 01 89. **Marketing:** through French merchants and foreign importers.

A perfume of oak undergrowth... a bouquet of blackcurrant leaves, fern, moss... velvet from the tannin... vanilla, *cachou,* cocoa, coffee... ever-changing sensations... The Bacqueys are not short of vocabulary to describe their wine, especially when they are talking of old vintages which with time have gained the necessary maturity and roundness, so that the good *crus* of Poujeaux can be drunk as they should be. This is not out of linguistic affectation; it is because the little property of Bel-Air Lagrave has for a long time featured on Moulis's roll of honour. It has been in the same family for one hundred and fifty years. Among its succession of owners we find the name of Adrien Dubois, manager of estates owned by the city of Bordeaux, as well as the Seguins, father and son, together estate managers of Château Bellegrave over a period of seventy years. The estate has only 9 hectares, run lovingly by the five Bacquey brothers and sisters who, together with their mother, are the present owners. They follow the old Médoc customs in everything: short pruning, long fermentation periods, and predominance of the cabernet. This gives a wine which is closed up when young, but superb when it has developed.

Bel-Air Lagrave has several distinguishing features. Firstly, in the nineteenth century the town of Saint Louis in the United States awarded its wine first prize: a rare

Jean-Paul, Arlette and Jocelyne Bacquey.

reward to which may be added all the gold, silver and bronze medals won since 1889 at the various exhibitions in Paris. Secondly, for twenty years it has kept a stock of bottles especially for private clients. So at the property today you can buy a 70, a 73 or a 76 if you have become rather weary of the 82s and 83s to be found everywhere else. This policy is to be applauded, for great wines may be good when they are young, but they are made to be drunk old. The example of Beaujolais Nouveau has created havoc even here in Bordeaux, and the wine is no sooner put in *barrique* before the so-called experts are analysing it in abstruse language. True drinkers are not taken in and leave to the press the curious foible of wanting to describe what the man will be like before the infant is even born. Of course, business has it laws and practices, and publicity is one of them, but I say to the customer, "Buy this wine and lay it down. Do not sabotage something that is still growing, needing several years to mature and harmonize five hundred constituent elements. And while you are waiting, drink a wine which has opened up, a Moulis 70, for example. It is beginning to be really delicious."

Bel-Air Lagrave's third distinguishing feature is that it is a wine made in accordance with the best of traditions. Despite their other occupations elsewhere, the people who make it are anxious to continue the work of their fathers and grandfathers. They have retained their love for their native soil, and they know how to speak to true lovers of wine.

Nearly every vintage of Bel-Air Lagrave confirms the authenticity of its tradition. This *cru* can take on any contender in its appellation in a blind tasting. Those who really know wine will always judge it among the best. It is truly a fine piece of work.

Bellegrave (Château)

Cru bourgeois

Commune: Listrac-Médoc. **Proprietor:** SC des Vignobles du Château Bellegrave, BP N° 4, Listrac-Médoc, 33480 Castelnau-de-Médoc. Managers: Jean-Louis Declercq and Henri Pètre. Consultant oenologist: Jacques Boissenot, Lamarque. **Size of vineyard:** 14.63 hectares. **Average age of vines:** 25 years. **Varieties:** 65% cabernet-sauvignon, 5% cabernet-franc, 25% merlot, 5% petit-verdot. **Production:** approx. 50,000 bottles CB. **Visits:** in July and August. Jean-Louis Declercq or Henri Pètre. Tel. 56 58 02 40. **Marketing:** by brokerage with sole rights for each country.

As there are eleven Château Bellegraves in the Gironde, care is needed not to confuse this one with the others. Bellegrave is one of the vineyards furthest to the north of Listrac in the hamlet of Couhenne, beside the railway, and not far from Cussac. It has two main parcels, one on the plateau of Les Marcieux, made up of limestone with clay and marl, and the other on a ridge of good Garonne gravel just by Château Beaumont. The estate was created in the last century and for a long time was run by the Mège family. Madame Jean Mège took an active part and was largely responsible for the fame of this *cru bourgeois*. After her, it passed into the hands of Lionel Hosteing, Monsieur Pécresse and then the Bordeaux merchant firm of Mestrézat-Merlaut.

Today Bellegrave is still owned by merchants, though Belgians, namely Messieurs Jean-Louis Declercq and Henri Pètre, in whose hands it has been since 1980. The fact that the proprietors are some distance away has not adversely affected the wine's quality. Four more hectares have been planted, adding rather more merlot to a wine which is typical of the cabernets. At a large tasting organized in Belgium for several great Bordeaux 84s, Bellegrave came out among the leaders just behind its neighbour Maucaillou and two excellent Margaux, Monbrison and Labégorce-Zédé. Jean-Louis Declercq, a friendly, good-natured man, is justifiably proud of this wine whose success has rewarded the dedication and enthusiasm which he and Henri Pètre have invested in it.

With harvesting by hand, two long fermentation periods, daily passing of the must over the marc, three-monthly rackings, fining with egg-whites and ageing for one and a half years in oak casks, the wine of Bellegrave is a classic both in its vinification and its quality. And if any doubt remained you would only need to listen to Jean-Louis Declercq on the subject; he is not short of words to describe the 83, one of the estate's great successes: "it is full-bodied, of great substance, with a clear note of the grapes' full maturity, aromas of resin, cedar and mint with a pronounced finish. It has breeding and is rich and voluptuous." In the wake of such a eulogy, we can only add that this wine won a silver medal at the *Salon de l'Agriculture* in Paris. Among recent vintages, it is the 88 which is the richest. Notable for its vinosity, its persistence and its opulence, which make it a remarkable wine, there is every reason to believe that it will age better than the 87 and the 89.

Bellevue-Laffont (Château)

→ *Fourcas-Dupré*

Bergeron (Château)

Cru bourgeois

Commune: Moulis-en-Médoc. **Proprietor:** Marie Bayonnette. Manager: Philippe Dourthe. Consultant oenologist: Château Duplessis-Fabre. **Size of vineyard:** 4.7 hectares. **Average age of vines:** 35 years. **Varieties:** 25% cabernet-sauvignon, 50% merlot, 13% malbec, 12% petit-verdot. **Production:** 4 *tonneaux,* 20,000 bottles CB. **Direct sales and by mail order:** in France. Marie Bayonnette, Château Bergeron, Moulis-en-Médoc, 33480 Castelnau-de-Médoc. Tel. 56 58 18 12.

This little Moulis vineyard, classed as a *cru bourgeois* in 1932, has four different grape varieties, including a proportion of old malbec vines. The Bergeron family owned and ran it at the beginning of the nineteenth century, then the Meyres. Raymond Bayonnette bought and ran the vineyard following his retirement from the merchant navy. After his death the Pagès leased the land for some time and now Philippe Dourthe has taken over the *cru:* this wine is as good as that of Duplessis-Fabre, which it resembles very closely.

Berthault-Brillette (Château)

→ *Brillette*

Biston-Brillette (Château)

Cru bourgeois

Commune: Moulis-en-Médoc. **Proprietor:** Michel Barbarin. Sales and marketing: Serge Barbarin. Cellar master: Jean-Paul Barbarin. **Size of vineyard:** 16 hectares. **Average age of vines:** 20 years. **Varieties:** 55% cabernet-sauvignon, 40% merlot, 3% malbec, 2% petit-verdot. **Production:** 60 *tonneaux,* 70,000 bottles CB. **Visits:** Monday to Friday from 8 a.m. to noon and 2 to 6 p.m. Michel Barbarin, tel. 56 58 22 86. **Direct sales and by mail order:** in France and abroad. Château Biston-Brillette, Moulis-en-Médoc, 33480 Castelnau-de-Médoc. **Marketing:** strictly to private clients.

Michel Barbarin is one of those men who give one confidence in the future of the wines of Moulis. His determination to make a wine of high quality is matched only by his dogged stamina in restoring his estate. When he came to Biston-Brillette in 1964 there was just one hectare of vines and one horse. That was a start, of course, but it was not much. So he set to work. Twenty years later the results speak for themselves: 18 hectares of impeccably kept vines under production, working buildings in first-class condition and faithful customers, won over by this grower's ability and his moderate prices. The part played by the family is also an engaging one. While Michel Barbarin prunes his vines, his wife looks after dispatching the orders, his elder son does the ploughing and the younger one works in the vat-house. There is no mystery attached to the present success of the estate, merely a great deal of hard work. With well-deserved results, it must be said.

Biston-Brillette is an old name, well known in the last century. The Menessier and Labrunie families owned it for a long time. There are some vines in the clayey limestone of Petit-Poujeaux and others on the gravelly ridge of Brillette. With three

Jean-Paul Barbarin spraying his young vines.

weeks' fermentation in stainless steel and two years in wood, it is a tannic, powerful and racy wine which should wait for ten to twenty years to develop a harmonious blend of aromas. The 78s and 79s are just beginning to open up and are superb. As with many of the *crus* from Moulis and Margaux, the 83s today seem better than the 82s and, because of their density, can keep for twenty-five years in the cellar without risk. Biston-Brillette is one of the most full-bodied of the Moulis wines, and in the French wine press tasters all praise it highly. If Monsieur Biston, the late-eighteenth-century grower who lived at Malmaison (in Moulis, not Napoleon's château), were to see all this from above he would be most pleased.

Do not confuse the wine-growing Biston-Brillette with château Biston, an elegant mansion in town which Monsieur and Madame Roux have converted into *chambres d'hôtes* and conference rooms. But they do not own a single vine there.

The only darker note was struck by the terrible January frost of 1985, which did not spare this estate. Michel Barbarin lost two hectares of cabernet when the thermometer dropped to – 20° C (– 4° F) for two nights running. This has reduced the amount of Biston-Brillette on the market, but it has not cooled the ardour of the proprietor or his customers. These are exclusively private clients, nearly all of whom the Barbarins know personally, whether restaurateurs or simply lovers of good wine. You are welcomed to the château as to a friend's home, and the wine is one to treat your best friends to – provided you give it time to develop.

Bouqueyran (Château)

Cru bourgeois

Commune: Moulis-en-Médoc. **Proprietor:** Pierre-Jean-Marie Martin. **Size of vineyard:** 7 hectares. **Varieties:** 40% cabernet-sauvignon, 5% cabernet-franc, 50% merlot, 5% petit-verdot. **Production:** 42,000 bottles. **Direct sales and by mail order:** in France and abroad. Château Bouqueyran, 33480 Moulis-en-Médoc. Tel. 56 88 84 70. **Marketing:** through the Bordeaux trade.

In the Moulis appellation there are comparatively few real châteaux in the architectural sense of the term. Bouqueyran is one of the rare ones to be able to claim this honour, by virtue of its size and its turreted slate roofs, which give it a very genteel and picturesque aspect.

At the beginning of the century it was a huge estate "comprising woods, meadows, land and a vineyard" and already classed as a *cru bourgeois supérieur* for the quality of its wine. Writers of the time stress "its excellence after fifteen or twenty years in the bottle". At that time the estate was in the hands of Louis Fronsac, a name seemingly predestined for wine makers, who produced forty *tonneaux* a year of red wine on the southern slope of the Puy-de-Menjon, as well as a white wine of high repute.

Bought in 1952 by Monsieur Martin, the property is run today by his grandson Jean-Marie. The total area of the vineyard has been reduced from what it once was, but under his care Bouqueyran is regaining its former place. This is only right and proper, for under the Ancien Régime, and even in the Middle Ages, the parish of "Bécoyran" was independent of the village of Moulis. The creation of communes after the Revolution and the subsequent demolition of the church modified its existence, but without affecting its long tradition of growing. This tradition deserves to be preserved, for the wines from Bouqueyran are an interesting synthesis of those from Moulis and from Listrac. The geological and geographical situation of their land makes them more like the Listracs, showing that the exact characteristics of all the Moulis AOC wines are far from easy to define; the more so because modern oenology and the vast increase in the use of new casks tend to balance out the typical flavour of the region, while sometimes enriching the wine in quite a spectacular way. A subsoil of 80% clayey limestone makes the wine of Château Bouqueyran both full-bodied and supple at the same time. Most of the wine is handled by the Bordeaux trade, but you can buy on the spot or by mail order.

Branas Grand Poujeaux (Château)

Commune: Moulis-en-Médoc. **Proprietor:** Jacques de Pourquery. Consultant oenologist: Monsieur Couasnon, Pauillac. **Size of vineyard:** 6 hectares. **Average age of vines:** 14 years. **Varieties:** 45% cabernet-sauvignon, 5% cabernet-franc, 40% merlot, 10% petit-verdot. **Production:** 40 *tonneaux,* 38,000 bottles CB. **Visits:** only by appointment with Jacques de Pourquery, tel. 56 58 03 07. **Direct sales and by mail order:** in France. Château Branas Grand Poujeaux, Moulis-en-Médoc, 33480 Castelnau-de-Médoc. **Marketing:** through Dutch, German, Swiss and Belgian merchants.

After buying it in 1963, Jacques de Pourquery patiently restored this little estate. He replanted cabernet and merlot on several parcels – on the pebbly ridge of Grand-Poujeaux and on more clayey land with subsoils of iron-pan. Thanks to him the name of Branas, an old Moulis growing family, lives on, as it deserves. Jean Branas, who comes back to the area from time to time, was for a long time one of the most eminent teachers at the agricultural college in Montpellier. He had as one of his pupils Dominique Hessel, who also became a grower at Moulis (see Moulin à Vent). And his father was estate manager at Duplessis Hauchecorne.

A sincere, dedicated grower who respects tradition as much as he respects his customers, Jacques de Pourquery makes a good wine, vinified and aged in the old style, which he sells to foreign merchants or direct at his cellars, which are open to visitors. His wine has won him several medals and it would be surprising if he did not win more, for Branas Grand Poujeaux is regularly and constantly improving. Jacques de Pourquery is also the owner of the little Clos des Demoiselles at Listrac. Small, round and jolly, he is one of the most pleasant and likeable figures in the appellation – and his wines resemble him.

Brillette (Château)

Commune: Moulis-en-Médoc. **Proprietor:** Monique Berthault. Cellar master: M. Crouzet. Consultant oenologist: Jacques Boissenot, Lamarque. **Size of vineyard:** 32 hectares. **Average age of vines:** 20 years. **Varieties:** 50% cabernet-sauvignon, 5% cabernet-franc, 40% merlot, 5% petit-verdot. **Production:** 180,000 bottles CB. **Visits:** from April to September, tel. 56 58 22 09. **Direct sales and by mail order:** in France. Château Brillette, Moulis-en-Médoc, 33480 Castelnau-de-Médoc. **Marketing:** through large chain stores and for export.

Brillette is a pretty, feminine, country name said to come from the glistening pebbles on the ridges that make up the estate. The vineyard faces south, so that the pebbles, silex, quartz and other minerals in the soil shine brilliantly in the sun. Brillette's wine owes its reputation to the age of the property and its distinct character. It was dubbed "ladies' wine" because of its lightness, delicacy and complete lack of aggressive tannins. It is also a lady's wine today because its owner, Madame Monique Berthault, is in complete charge, and one of the few women growers in the Moulis and Listrac AOCs.

In the nineteenth century Brillette belonged to the extensive estates of the Comtes du Périer de Larsan. Together with the nearby Château Barreyres at Arcins, it represented a huge viticultural empire for this family, and from 1850 Brillette, which produced thirty *tonneaux* annually, was one of the best *crus* in the commune. The estate then had various ups and downs, changing hands several times, and its production was considerably reduced, for in 1960 it had only three hectares of vines. Raymond Berthault, an outstanding personality in the world of French chain stores,

Monique Berthault, a dedicated grower.

the founder and chairman of Viniprix and Euromarché, bought Brillette in 1976. He immediately gave his estate a new impetus which within a few years completely reversed the decline in fortune that it had suffered. Since the death of her husband in 1981, Madame Berthault has continued his work. A woman of character, very enthusiastic about wine and extremely ambitious for her *cru*, she has administered the estate with great ability and in a highly individual way, her methods sometimes contrasting strongly with those of her neighbours. But the memory of her husband lives on at Moulis and his name is still linked to it through a second label, Château Berthault-Brillette.

The wine of château Brillette is always well balanced, rather supple, smooth and generally elegant. Its lightness does not detract from the hints of raspberry and cherry for which its adherents know and love it. Of recent vintages the 79, 81 and 82 are of very high quality and reflect the traditional charm of this old *cru bourgeois*. The 85 follows along in the same tradition. Harvesting is done by machine and the wine, rich in aromas, mellow and fine like all the great Moulis, ages for eighteen months in wooden *barriques*. Part is distributed by the Bordeaux trade and goes for export, but Brillette sells to private customers either by mail order or directly from the château.

Wine-lovers may discover the unmistakable terrain of the *croupe de Brillette* when the château is open to visitors from April to September. The soil holds up well in comparison with that of its neighbour Grand Poujeaux, which is similar in geological make-up. This similitary manifests itself particulary clearly in great years.

Cantegric (Château) 🛡

→ *Liouner*

Cap de Haut-Maucaillou (Château) 🛡 → *Maucaillou*

Capdet (Château)

Commune: Listrac-Médoc. **Proprietor:** Monsieur David Raymond, Ludeye, Listrac-Médoc, 33480 Castelnau-de-Médoc. Tel. 56 58 00 96. Tenant: Jean-Marie Raymond. **Size of vineyard:** 8 hectares. **Average age of vines:** 20 years. **Varieties:** 42% cabernet-sauvignon, 10% cabernet-franc, 48% merlot. **Production:** 40 *tonneaux*. **Marketing:** vinification at Listrac's *cave coopérative, tel 56 58 03 19.*

Château Capdet has been in existence for a long time; in 1920 Raymond *grand-père* was already producing thirty *tonneaux* on his little estate. Today the vineyard is still in the same family, but David Raymond takes his harvest to the *coopérative* at Listrac to be vinified. It is a pity that, with 8 hectares of fully mature vines with a preponderance of merlot, this old name cannot assert a more distinct personality. But the Capdet label certainly does not disgrace the others at the *coopérative*. On the contrary, it is continuing the tradition of the *vins de châteaux,* that is of *crus* which are vinified in a *coopérative* while retaining some degree of autonomy.

Cap Léon Veyrin (Château)

Commune: Listrac-Médoc. **Proprietor:** Alain Meyre. Consultant oenologist: Jacques Boissenot, Lamarque. **Size of vineyard:** 18 hectares. **Average age of vines:** 15 years. **Varieties:** 50% cabernet-sauvignon, 50% merlot. **Production:** 100 *tonneaux,* 80,000 to 100,000 bottles CB. **Visits:** weekdays from 9 a.m. to noon and 2 to 7 p.m. Sundays, by appointment. Tel. 56 58 07 28. **Direct sales and by mail order:** in France and abroad. Château Cap Léon Veyrin, Listrac-Médoc, 33480 Castelnau-de-Médoc. **Marketing:** 30% for export, the rest to private clients.

"Lou Cap"in local dialect means "head"; Léon is the name of a former proprietor at Donissan. Champ de Cap Léon is a parcel of land which has always been on the land register at Listrac. And Veyrin is another parcel, first known as Veyrin-

Château Cap Léon Veyrin, perfect for a Christmas card.

Domecq, a vineyard belonging to the Delbos family, proprietors of Lanessan, at the beginning of the century. Hence the derivation of this unusual name, made up of words which are rather uncommon in this region. What is even more unusual is that this Cap has been in the same family since 1810. First of all came the Curats in the nineteenth century, then the Meyres, when the two brothers, Antoine and Jean, married the two Curat sisters, Zélia and Elina. In short, a clear-cut succession in a line as direct and straight as Jules-Irénée Meyre himself, now approaching his eightieth year. He is a cattle-dealer, like all the Meyres from Listrac, and a skilled grower.

If you want to know anything about Listrac, do not hesitate to ask Jules-Irénée Meyre. His reminiscences stretch back over seventy years and his memory is as sound as a bell. No one else can tell local stories the way he does. For example: "To avoid the merchants diluting the wine, I was one of the first to bottle every drop of my wine round about 1930. Everybody in the village said, 'That twit Irénée wants to drink all his wine himself!' In fact, with us, wine is like a member of the family and we respect it."

Fortunately this respect is hereditary, for today Alain Meyre, his son, makes one of the appellation's best wines. The vines are on different terrains: clayey-limestone at the top of Cap Léon, and marly gravel over by Peyrelebade. The vinification

period is long and marries traditional and modern practices. The wine remains in wood for a year and the *barriques* are renewed yearly. The care taken at this stage of its development, together with the differences in soil and the blend of grapes, give the wine of Château Cap Léon Veyrin an exceptionally long life. The 29s, 37s and 45s, religiously preserved in the family "vault", are living proof of this, not to mention the 47s and the 61s. Nearer our own day, all the vintages have been successful from the elegant 78 to the robust 86, both equally fruity. It should be mentioned that the 81 was selected by the Conseil interprofessionnel du vin de Bordeaux to promote Listrac wines in general, and that the very powerful 82 will doubtless have reached its peak round about the year 2000.

Another attraction of this estate is that the Meyres have *chambres d'hôte* available. Guests may visit the cellars before sitting down to eat a home-made *confit* with a bottle of old wine. An ever-increasing number of faithful customers know this worthwhile vineyard, particularly appreciated, incidentally by Marisa Berenson while making the film *"Flagrant désir"* at nearby Cussac! Cap Léon Veyrin is an excellent example of a family concern which has astutely developed a side-line in authentic tourism while preserving local growing traditions. Its wine does the appellation honour and every wine lover should have some in his cellar, for it is one of the most typical and best made of the Listracs. There is a newcomer among the labels of Alain Meyre: Château Julien, made from vines recently acquired in Cussac.

Caroline (Château)  → Lestage

Chasse-Spleen (Château)

Cru exceptionnel

Commune: Moulis-en-Médoc. **Proprietor:** SC du Château Chasse-Spleen. Administrator and estate manager: Bernadette Villars. Vineyard manager: Robert Chabot. Cellar master: Eric Sirac. Consultant oenologist: Jacques Boissenot, Lamarque. **Size of vineyard:** 65 hectares. **Average age of vines:** 25 years. **Varieties:** 55% cabernet-sauvignon, 3% cabernet-franc, 35% merlot, 7% petit-verdot. **Production:** 350,000 bottles CB. **Visits:** Monday to Friday, by appointment only. Mme Bernadette Villars, tel. 56 58 02 37. **Sales by mail order:** in France. Château Chasse-Spleen, Grand Poujeaux, Moulis, 33480 Castelnau-de-Médoc. **Marketing:** in the traditional way, *en primeur,* through the brokers and the Bordeaux trade.

"Wine conjures up many a magic doorway in its exhalations, gold and red like a sunset in a hazy sky." Did Baudelaire drink Chasse-Spleen or not? Bernadette Villars, in charge of this magnificent estate today, would like to be able to prove it, recapturing the symbolist's *"spleen"*, his melancholia, and recording his profession of faith on an advertising leaflet. "I have more memories than if I were a thousand years old." Chasse-Spleen is a long way from counting an existence of a thousand years. The property results from the splitting up of the Gressier family's assets at the beginning of the nineteenth century. A Gressier daughter married a wealthy man called Castaing who traded with France's Caribbean colonies. Legend has it that it was Lord Byron himself who christened the wine "Chasse-Spleen" (literally "chase away the blues") after drinking a few glasses in 1821. No documentary evidence supports this claim. In fact, Château Chasse-Spleen's rise to fame is relatively recent.

Tastings often take place in the cellars of Chasse-Spleen.

At the very beginning of this century it was in the hands of a German wine-merchant, Segnitz from Brême. In 1914 it was confiscated as "assets belonging to the enemy" and Frank Lahary, a native of the Landes *département*, bought it in 1922. It is certainly he who is responsible for the *cru*'s excellent reputation today.

Even though it figures among the *crus bourgeois* of the Médoc, Chasse-Spleen has been generally considered as a *cru classé* partly because of its quality and also because of the strong market demand for this renowned wine. Therefore it is generally proposed at higher prices than the other *bourgeois* to the Bordeaux trade during the traditional spring *primeur* campaign.

Two-thirds of the vineyard are situated on the two fine gravelly ridges of Grand-Poujeaux and Granins, planted mainly with cabernet-sauvignon. The remaining third is clayey limestone planted with merlot. The final balance of this combination gives the wine a fullness which makes Chasse-Spleen one of the most powerful and full-bodied of all the wines of the Médoc. Over the last ten years it has often been among the leaders at blind tastings which have included several great *crus classés*. What I find even more remarkable is its outstanding early maturity in the great years and, at the same time, the wine's consistently high quality; "off-years" such as 1980 or 1984 are more than commendable. But I think the best of all is the 1982 which promises to be a very, very great bottle. I will call on Baudelaire once more to describe it:

> "Its harmony is perfect bliss,
> Its elegance we laud;
> And futile all analysis
> To name each wondrous chord."

B.G.

Chemin Royal (Château)

Cru bourgeois

Commune: Moulis-en-Médoc. **Proprietor:** SCI Château Fonréaud, Listrac-Médoc, 33480 Castelnau-de-Médoc. **Size of vineyard:** 4 hectares. **Average age of vines:** 21 years. **Varieties:** 35% cabernet-sauvignon, 65% merlot. **Production:** 26 *tonneaux,* 30,000 bottles CB. **Visits:** from 8 a.m. to noon and 2 to 5.30 p.m. at Château Fonréaud. Tel. 56 58 02 43. **Marketing:** through the Bordeaux trade.

Already firmly established at Listrac with Lestage and Fonréaud, the Chanfreau family has a sort of third child in Chemin Royal, though rather different from its elders because it comes from Moulis. It is two parcels of land totalling four hectares on the heights of Bouqueyran, just behind Moulin à Vent. This soil is typical of Moulis, with a mixture of pebbles from the Pyrenees and clayey limestone, which suits the grape varieties perfectly.

There is every reason to believe that under the Ancien Régime, Chemin Royal belonged to Château Mauvezin. It certainly belonged to the Le Blanc family at Mauvezin for a long time. One of them, called Clément-Hyppolite, bought it from his brothers and sisters in 1831. His son became proprietor of Fonréaud in 1858 and so united the destiny of the two estates which were bought by Monsieur Chanfreau in 1962. The vineyard began to be replanted in 1966, at which time it produced only trade a small quantity of wine, little known and distributed only through the Bordeaux trade. Over recent years, the wines of Chemin Royal have been given the closest attention by Jean Chanfreau, who has introduced a small amount of new wood into the ageing process. Recent vintages, in particular the 83, are very harmonious and well-balanced. The predominating merlot makes the wine supple with attractive hints of fruit and spices. The 85s and 86s, concentrated and tannic, are unquestionably suitable for laying down.

But this wine does not require ten years to open up: it can be drunk relatively young. The lack of pretentiousness and agressive bite makes Chemin Royal an excellent luncheon wine whose tannins are generally well absorbed.

Clarke (Château)

Cru bourgeois supérieur

Commune: Listrac-Médoc. **Proprietor:** Compagnie Vinicole des Barons Edmond et Benjamin de Rothschild. Sales and marketing director: Denis Edange. Director General: Jean-Claude Boniface. Cellar master: Philippe Bonnin. Consultant oenologist: Monsieur Jacques Boissenot, à Lamarque. **Size of vineyard:** 132 hectares. **Average age of vines:** fifteen years. **Varieties:** 41.5% cabernet-sauvignon, 11% cabernet-franc, 45% merlot, 2.5% petit-verdot. **Production:** 300,000 bottles CB. **Visits:** Mademoiselle Pascale Cayre, by appointment only, tel. 56 88 84 29. **Direct sales and by mail order:** in France and for export. Compagnie Vinicole des Barons Edmond et Benjamin de Rothschild, Château Clarke, 33480 Listrac-Médoc. Tel. 56 88 88 00.

Hunting trophies and a Roman wine seller's sign in Clarke's cellar.

Like the investments represented by the purchase of Château Lagrange in Saint-Julien or even Château Margaux, the creation of Château Clarke at Listrac was one of the most spectacular bets that could have been made on the future of the Médoc. With a yearly injection of ten million francs for twelve years in order to bring this estate back to life, Baron de Rothschild's intentions were misinterpreted at first. The incredulous asked "How can a Rothschild come and settle in Listrac, on unpromising land in a commune which does not have the prestige of the great appellations?" Clearly, they thought, his cousins had chosen better. "But whatever is he going to do at Listrac? Certainly not make a great wine." In short, speculation was rife; people were sceptical and mocked. They would have done better to wait to judge from the results. For they were wrong, and we shall see why.

At first there was a vast plateau, half clay, half stones, stretching to the east of the village of Listrac and to the north of Moulis. In the Middle Ages, Cistercian monks were said to have come to cultivate a few vines and a little wheat. The land was dependent on the Abbey of Vertheuil, later passing under the control of the barony of Blanquefort. In 1771 a knight of Irish origin called Tobie Clarke arrived in Listrac. His family fled from Ireland in the seventeenth century, after supporting the Catholic party of King James II in his struggle with William of Orange. After the latter's victory at the battle of Drogheda, the old Catholic families emigrated from the island, more often than not coming to Nantes and Bordeaux. Clarke, who lived in the rue des Menuts in the parish of Saint-Michel in Bordeaux, paid 94,000 livres tournois for the estate, then called Les Granges, which covered about 230 hectares. 107

Château Clarke has come back to life...

The previous proprietor, who also lived in the vicinity of Saint-Michel, but in the rue Leyteire, had had a considerable number of buildings constructed, in particular "a vat-house also serving as a cellar", as the deeds stipulated. A professional ship-owner, Clarke died in Listrac only eight months after buying Les Granges. His son, a lawyer and later judge of appeal in Bordeaux, inherited it and lived there for several years. Quite naturally, the property took the name of Château Clarke from the nineteenth century. From the 17 hectares of vines in existence in 1818, the average harvest produced 18 *tonneaux*. But Luc Clarke's death created problems and the estate was sold at auction on August 21, 1821. The Saint-Guirons family became its owners and in 1865 had the château built in the eclectic neo-classical style of Napoleon III. The first labels on bottles of Clarke have a picture of this edifice. The family ran the estate for a long time, then it was handed down by inherit-ance, generally through the female line – Madame Abiet, Antoine Saint-Guirons's daughter, Madame Merman, Madame Cantegril, the wife of the mayor of Listrac, and Madame John-Durand, their daughter. So we come to the year 1955, in which Georges Bidon bought a château in ruins and 80 hectares of land. Things went badly: the château had to be demolished and the vineyard grew smaller and smaller. Château Clarke was beginning its time in the wilderness.

Edmond de Rothschild arrived in 1973 and paid four and a half million francs for a run-down estate. Today, after the acquisition of the adjacent estate of Peyrelebade in 1979 (see below), the Baron has 173 hectares, of which 150 have been completely replanted. These figures show the extent to which the estate has been brought back to

and is now a superb viticultural estate.

life. Many others could be quoted: Clarke's vat-house has thirty-three ultra-modern stainless steel vats; drainage necessitated the creation of some 15 kilometres of ditch; pruning occupies eighteen people for four months; there is a hectare of gardens containing five hundred rose trees, not counting, of course those planted at the end of the vine rows, in accordance with Gironde tradition. A lover of trees, Edmond de Rothschild has had dozens planted in the park. A lime tree, already sixty years old, was brought specially from Holland by lorry to cast its shade over the terrace. In 1973 Clarke consisted of by three buildings in ruins and a derelict shed; ten years later a thriving business had taken its place.

Pierre Saintout, president of the Viticultural Federation of Listrac, who died in August 1984, was Clarke's first director, and the first to understand what incomparable prestige his appellation could gain from Baron Edmond's huge investment. Now that the early, legitimate doubts are over, all Listrac's growers recognize that a Rothschild is one of the best possible leading lights they could have. Along with this, Pierre Saintout created one of Clarke's great distinguishing features by managing each parcel of land separately. The vineyard has been divided into 114 parcels and each one is managed individually. The climate, soil, yield, grape varieties, fertilizers, pruning and the rest are computerized, and the wine's quality is assessed regularly by a committee of experts: Professor Peynaud, the oenologist Jacques Boissenot and (until his resignation in 1989) Gérard Colin, the manager of the Compagnie Vinicole des Barons Edmond et Benjamin (his son) de Rothschild. In view of the 'high-tech' approach which reigns here, it comes as no surprise that a special drain-laying machine, the only one in the world, was constructed especially for Clarke. Four metres high and ten metres long, it moves on caterpillar tracks. Thus, highly sophisticated technology has come to serve vine-growing. Such is progress.

In the face of such advances Clarke's first vintages were rather dull. But the estate's oldest vines were only five years old in 1978. Not until 1982, in fact, did the wine reach a quality worthy of its proprietor's hopes. Starting with this vintage, Clarke's general standard rose rapidly. Of course the 81 is good but, dominated by the cabernet on chalky soil, it remains very woody and has a rather dry finish. The 82 is delicious, being fuller, richer and more fruity. The 83 confirmed this progress; it is round and has a great deal of charm. But it is the 85 which I find exceptional. Towards the mid-1990s (and much later) it will certainly be a prodigious wine. "Yes, it is good, but it is expensive", moans the consumer, rather disheartened by the price of a bottle of Clarke (the most expensive of all the Listracs) when he wants to buy three cases. Obviously when you invest millions in an AOC wine, it is not to sell it in bulk to the trade at five francs a litre! Whether in Pauillac, Sauternes or Listrac, the Rothschilds are not in the habit of selling their products cut-price, for they are generally at the top of the range. It seems that when you buy a bottle of Clarke, you pay at once for the wine, the label and the unusual story of the *cru*'s rebirth. Without wanting to make a false comparison, we should remember that when Baron Philippe (Edmond's cousin) came to Mouton-Rothschild in the twenties, he provoked many gibes with decisions which were at the time considered outrageous. But one generation was sufficient to make Mouton an important site, not only viticulturally but also artistically and culturally, known the world over and quite unique.

Clarke is following along these lines; Edmond de Rothschild has simply wanted to make an appointment with the future. He is said to be an astute financier and remarkable businessman, so it is not difficult to imagine what Clarke will be like in the year 2000, for example. Then, the estate will have attained the cruising speed it is aiming for today, particularly as regards marketing. Experience, reputation and the age of the vines will have had their effect. New measures, already planned today, will have spread the label's fame in other areas (the arts, for example). In short, Clarke is only in its adolescence. But when it has become an adult, we shall be able to doff our hats to the ability to create something great out of nothing.

Decorde (Château)

→ *Sémeillan-Mazeau*

Demoiselles (Clos des)

Commune: Listrac-Médoc. **Proprietor:** Jacques de Pourquery. **Size of vineyard:** 4 hectares. **Average age of vines:** 14 years. **Varieties:** 60% cabernet-sauvignon, 35% merlot, 5% petit-verdot. **Production:** 20 *tonneaux,* 20,000 bottles CB. **Visits:** daily. Micheline Augeau, tel. 56 58 05 12. **Direct sales and by mail order:** in France and abroad. Clos des Demoiselles, Listrac-Médoc, 33480 Castelnau-de-Médoc. **Marketing:** foreign sales; Holland, Germany, Belgium, Switzerland.

With another property in Moulis, Jacques de Pourquery also owns this little vineyard in the shadow of the fire watchtower at the top of Puy-de-Menjon on the way into Listrac. It is marked by a building at the side of the road almost opposite Fonréaud, with flags draped like banners all round it, announcing to tourists that his wine travels all over Europe. They can stop here too, for this little house is actually a very charming sales and tasting centre.

Descendant of a Périgord family, Jacques de Pourquery married a girl from Listrac, and this vineyard (one of the smallest in the commune) came to him through his in-laws, who had owned it since 1820 according to the deeds. It took its name from the little locality where it is situated, for "Les Demoiselles" was once the place where the pretty young girls of the parish were presented to the important personages of the Ancien Régime when they passed through the village. Thus the municipal land register has recorded the memory of these virtuous maidens honoured in regal fashion, and Jacques de Pourquery has created a charming label which is both virginal and Virgilian. Equally charming is the proprietor, whose meticulous care is exemplary. Because of its small size the Clos des demoiselles can not claim the title of *cru bourgeois,* but its quality is certainly at this level.

The land is of siliceous clay with a subsoil of gravel facing directly south, giving early ripening and a well-balanced wine for long keeping. The 79s, 80s and 81s have now opened up. More recent vintages deserve to wait a while, especially because since 1985 the proprietor has started using a high proportion of new wood to age his wine. The dominant cabernet gives these "Demoiselles" extra elegance. "It is a wine of great character," says Jacques de Pourquery, who finds it "very fruity, generous and delicate". He is not afraid of blowing his own trumpet.

Donissan (Château)

Cru bourgeois

Commune: Listrac-Médoc. **Proprietors:** brothers Roger and Jean Laporte in family trust. Consultant oenologist: Pierre Bariteau, Castelnau-de-Médoc. **Size of vineyard:** 7 hectares. **Average age of vines:** 25 years. **Varieties:** 47% cabernet-sauvignon, 48% merlot, 5% petit-verdot. **Production:** 30 to 40 *tonneaux.* **Visits:** by appointment preferably. Roger and Jean Laporte, tel. 56 58 04 77. **Direct sales and by mail order:** in France. Château Donissan, Listrac-Médoc, 33480 Castelnau-de-Médoc. **Marketing:** through the trade.

Donissan is one of the Médoc's oldest noble houses, which thrived under the Ancien Régime. Only a very few traces of its illustrious history remain, but from time to time deep ploughing at the top of Cap Léon brings to light stones which could well be the foundations of an old château. Moreover local tradition, handed down by word of mouth, tells rather vaguely of a fortified château at Donissan some time in the distant past. The same legend also tells of barques sailing from the estuary to this little hamlet, travelling along brooks and channels which were then wider than they are today. It is this tenuous relationship with maritime life which is responsible for the picture of a sailing-boat on the label of Listrac's *coopérative*. It could well be true, for throughout the Middle Ages the Médoc was a land of watercourses, marshes and canals. Barges could certainly have found a way inland between two ridges, and Listrac's topographical position would certainly seem to support this assumption.

What is much more certain, however, is the existence of a chapel at Donissan. It too was demolished a very long time ago (like the one at Bouqueyran) but several sarcophagi have been discovered. Naturally enough, they were used as drinking-troughs for cattle! During the Revolution the Marquis of Donissan, a vassal of the lord of Citran, his neighbour, had his lands seized. His daughter was bitterly resentful and, like many noble families in the area, took revenge by taking part with her husband in uprisings in the Vendée. This loyalty to the crown cost them dear, but it is said that she bore her troubles with determination and fortitude. Does this spirit still survive today in the pride with which Donissan claims to be independent of the village of Listrac, on which it in fact depends? For true natives Donissan is their village and Listrac is another and quite separate one. If you accidentally get it wrong, they will set the dogs on you. Take my word for it and do not play with fire. Everyone has his pride, and the inhabitants of Donissan undeniably have more than most.

Compared with this pride, which is sincerely felt and, it would seem, justified by history, the Château Donissan of today seems rather dull: a modest farm with a cowshed next to the cellar, and jet-black Friesians grazing amid the mounds of discarded grape-stalks. It is a family smallholding which has come down to the La-porte brothers, who cultivate 7 hectares of vines in different parcels. In comparison with the site's long aristocratic tradition, the wine seems rather plebeian, reflecting the permanence of this viticulture which has never accepted change easily, and into which modern oenology enters by carefully measured steps. But a little effort in this direction would give the wine a bit more brilliance.

Ducluzeau (Château)

Commune: Listrac-Médoc. **Proprietor:** Mme Jean-Eugène Borie. Vineyard managers: André Faure and Louis Lalanne. Cellar master: René Lusseau. Consultant oenologist: Emile Peynaud. **Size of vineyard:** 4 hectares. **Average age of vines:** 30 years. **Varieties:** 10% cabernet-sauvignon, 90% merlot. **Production:** 20 *tonneaux,* 20,000 bottles CB. **Marketing:** through Bordeaux and Maison Coste in Langon.

This little vineyard of four hectares produces perhaps the most "feminine" of Listrac wines, for two reasons. The first derives from the choice of grapes – 90% merlot, giving a delicacy and grace which are in contrast to the usual virility of the Listrac *crus*. The second derives from its history, for Ducluzeau has almost always been handed on through the female line, down to the present owner, Madame J.-E. Borie. And yet the first known owner was a man, Monsieur Ducluzeau. The *cru*, which has existed since the eighteenth century, was sold in 1870 to Monsieur Astien, a grower from Moulis who came to live in Listrac after marrying one of the Hugon daughters. They settled in the little locality of Le Mayne in the attractive house we see on the label. They had a daughter who became the wife of André Rochette. And Monique Rochette, their daughter, married Jean-Eugène Borie, vintner not only of the good merlot of Ducluzeau but also of Ducru-Beaucaillou, Haut-Batailley, Grand-Puy-Lacoste and Lalande-Borie. This proved a godsend for this fine wine, which for over forty years had lost its identity in the vats of the *cave coopérative*. It found its own label again only in 1976, and Jean-Eugène Borie's talents as a wine maker are sufficiently well known to make it unecessary for us to point out that it has fallen into excellent hands.

Aged for six months in oak and fined with albumen, the wine comes from different parcels which are impeccably kept, some of then lying on the highest gravelly land in Listrac. The vines are pruned and lovingly cared for by Louis Lalanne, who still makes his own supporting stakes. His mother, who has lived on the property since 1934, can recite the family tree of several families in the village without getting a single Christian name wrong. She knows the area inside out, for she has travelled all over it by bicycle for fifty years. An amusing detail: when André Rochette bought a house in Castelnau in 1930, the seller proved to be a Monsieur Ducluzeau, a distant relative of the original grower. Even today, several Ducluzeau families all over France are anxious to have a few bottles of the wine which bears their name, so as to be able to impress their friends.

Because of its recent reappearance and its slender production, Ducluzeau is relatively little known. Accordingly, it does not have the status it deserves – a place it occupied in the nineteenth century when it was considered one of the best in Listrac. Like the other wines from the area, it needs time to reach its peak but you can begin to drink the 1982, a magnificent wine, rich and round without the hard finish of more recent vintages, which are still austere, though of outstanding promise. On the other hand, the 79 is beginning to be superb, with a splendid nose, power, elegance and fine fruit aromas. The 83 rather resembles it but you should not open it before the early 1990s. You will be handsomely rewarded for your patience. At the beginning of the century Ducluzeau was exported to Russia, where it had established an excellent reputation. Today it travels as far as the South Pole, for in 1985 marine engineers opened a bottle of 83 when they were on an expedition there. They wrote to Jean-Eugène Borie, thanking him for having warmed them up so well.

Duplessis Fabre (Château)

Commune: Moulis-en-Médoc. **Proprietor:** SCA des Domaines Château Maucaillon. Manager: Monsieur Philippe Dourthe. Vineyard manager: Maurice Bodin. Cellar master: Jean-Marc Gobineau. Consultant oenologist: Jacques Boissenot, Lamarque. **Size of vineyard:** 18 hectares. **Average age of vines:** 18 years. **Varieties:** 42% cabernet-sauvignon, 8% cabernet-franc, 50% merlot. **Production:** 85 *tonneaux,* 90,000 bottles CB. **Visits:** tel. 56 58 01 23. **Direct sales and by mail order:** in France. SCA des Domaines du Château Maucaillou, 33480 Moulis-en-Médoc. **Marketing:** Sold directly for export and through representatives in France.

Louis François Armand de Vignerot du Plessis, Duc de Richelieu, Marshal of France and Governor of Guienne, was a great man in every sense of the word. He is attributed with a positively incalculable number of escapades and conquests both in love and war. But although he was imprisoned during his youth for his intransigent and dissolute ways, he was also an academician and patron of the arts. It is to him we owe the Grand Théâtre in Bordeaux, the designs for which he commissioned from the architect Victor Louis. Great-nephew of the notorious cardinal, a fierce opponent of the English and a redoubtable confiscator of booty, this gentleman-bandit made his mark on the eighteenth century. How could he not have been a wine lover?

He was so fond of it that, naturally enough, he owned vines in the Médoc. His property in Moulis had been built in the seventeenth century and, apart from being a vineyard, it also served as a hunting lodge. In view of the reputation of the marshal and governor, mischievous tongues claimed that this lodge had quite another purpose and that, being so fond of hunting, he did a great deal of fishing of a differ-

The Cazali household with Jean Crété, their partner.

114

ent sort too. Let us pass discretly by. In the nineteenth century its history became more serious and Château Duplessis became the property of two brothers-in-law, both wine-brokers, Léon Favre and Alcide Hauchecorne. There was a good vineyard of 84 hectares, carefully tended by the two proprietors and planted on land of marly clay. But later the two brothers-in-law divided the estate in two, each having an equal share, one half being called Duplessis Fabre (not Favre – the result of a classic phonetic change) and the other Duplessis Hauchecorne, and from that time each became entirely separate.

Today Château Duplessis Fabre has 25 hectares of mainly young vines. When it was bought by Guy Pagès in 1974 (see Fourcas Dupré), only 0.7 hectares were in production. Guy Pagès had a pioneer's confidence, and he progressively replanted five different parcels. The result was a total rebirth of the estate. The buildings (cellar, vat-house and dwelling) have been patiently restored in the middle of an attractive park, in which nature plane-trees and century-old walnut-trees bear witness to the estate's noble origins.

In 1989 Duplessis Fabre was bought by Philippe Dourthe, owner of Château Maucaillou, who needed only to cross the village of Moulis to get to his new vineyard. Although the terrain here is very different from that of Grand Poujeaux, Philippe Dourthe fell in love with this estate at first sight and within twenty-four hours made up his mind to purchase it. Several months later he became the president of Moulis's viticultural Federation, and today this enterprising grower is the largest proprietor in the commune, for he owns nearly 15% of the land with the right to the Moulis appellation. Duplessis Fabre is a typical Moulis in its colour, bouquet and charm. Practically every vintage since 1975 has won a medal, a justifiable reward for a high-class product. Well-bred, well-balanced and generally full of body, it is a wine which is highly suitable for ageing, but it is also very good when young, with aromas of fruit and well-absorbed tannin.

Duplessis Hauchecorne (Château)

Commune: Moulis-en-Médoc. **Proprietor:** SC des Grands Crus réunis. Manager: Lucien Lurton. Consultant oenologist: Jacques Boissenot, Lamarque. **Size of vineyard:** 17.5 hectares. **Average age of vines:** 25 years. **Varieties:** 65% cabernet-sauvignon, 20% merlot, 10% malbec, 5% petit-verdot. **Production:** 96,000 bottles CB. **Marketing:** Ets Mestrezat-Preller, cours de la Martinique, 33000 Bordeaux.

This is the other Duplessis, the one belonging to the Bordeaux broker named Hauchecorne, who did so much for its reputation and whom we have already met in the preceding *cru*. As it has almost the same name as Duplessis Fabre, you might think that this Duplessis resembles it. Not a bit of it. Known at the beginning of the century by the name of Duplessis-Haut Vignoble, it had more than 30 hectares, giving a production of 100 *tonneaux*. Under the care of Alcide Hauchecorne and then later the firm of Delor, this estate became one of the foremost in the commune. It was also Monsieur Delor who had the present buildings constructed in Les Chalets, on the road linking the hamlet of Bouqueyran to the village of Moulis.

In the twentieth century the estate has seen many changes and in particular lost part of its vineyard. Today it is Lucien Lurton, one of the largest proprietors in the Bordeaux region (his properties include Brane-Cantenac, Bouscaut, Durfort-Vivens and Climens among others), who owns Duplessis-Hauchecorne's 18 hectares, split into two parcels, one round the "château", and the other on the fringe of the Listrac appellation, whose soil of clayey limestone resembles that of its neighbours Lestage and Clarke. It should be noted that the petit-verdot and malbec represent 15% of the total *encépagement* of Duplessis and that several rows of old vines give the wine a fine bouquet and delicacy. It is however very different from its similarly named neighbour Duplessis-Fabre. The wine is maybe less delicate, a little harsher, very full-bodied and bulkier. Similar to a Listrac because of its soil, it also shares its characteristic hardiness, which gives it a good potential for longevity.

Ageing, moreover, lasts for a year, in casks from Château Brane-Cantenac, a fact which since 1983 has helped to restore some of this label's former prestige. In January 1985 frost attacked the vineyard mercilessly, and as a result a great amount of work has been done to improve drainage and vines have been extensively replanted. The wine of Duplessis Hauchecorne rarely attains the peaks of perfection as regards elegance and quality, but is always reliable and unpretentious. Yet we would be justified in expecting rather better of a wine bearing the respected Lurton name. It is to be hoped that it will always be worthy of the verse painted in red on the walls of the vat-house:

> "Cru bourgeois supérieur, Duplessis-Hauchecorne,
> For more than a century its perfumes enthral
> In a wine, cool and heady, which gourmets ne'er scorn –
> Nor you, nor your friends, in euphoria's pall."

Dutruch Grand Poujeaux (Château)

Commune: Moulis-en-Médoc. **Proprietor:** François Cordonnier. Consultant oenologist: Jacques Boissenot, Lamarque. **Size of vineyard:** 25 hectares. **Average age of vines:** 30 years. **Varieties:** 40% cabernet-sauvignon, 15% cabernet-franc, 35% merlot, 10% petit-verdot. **Production:** 110 *tonneaux*. **Visits:** by appointment only. Madame Cordonnier, tel. 56 58 02 55. **Direct sales and by mail order:** in France. Château Dutruch Grand Poujeaux, Moulis-en-Médoc, 33480 Castelnau-de-Médoc. **Marketing:** foreign sales through the trade.

The line of ownership could not be simpler. First of all there was the founder, old Monsieur Dutruch, then there was the Lambert family, and now there is François Cordonnier. This is an old Moulis vineyard, having little history but whose reputation is firmly established, enjoying particular success in Belgium: gold medals were won in Brussels and Ghent before the First World War. This estate has a striking, serenity firmly rooted in history. François Cordonnier's mild character perhaps contributes to this. The grandson and great-grandson of wine merchants in Lille, he settled in Moulis in 1967 after being in charge of the famous château at Chenonceaux, whose wines are less familiar than its arches across the river Loire. But heredity and the vineyard of Chenonceaux have together helped François Cordonnier to settle in this vine-growing region with ease.

Planted in the old manner (ten thousand plants per hectare), the vines are spread out over various parcels in the gravelly soils of Grand-Poujeaux and the clayey limestone nearer the village of Moulis. They are a perfect example of how vineyards should be, and contain many old vines whose influence is reflected in the deep colour of the wine. It ages for eighteen months, sometimes in new casks, sometimes in oval

Monsieur and Madame Cordonnier.

A symbolic bas-relief.

oak *foudres*, those immense casks so much in favour at one time but now becoming rarer and rarer in the Médoc. One more trace of the past is to be found on the door of the cellar, which is decorated with a charming sculpture depicting bunches of grapes. We chose this bas-relief with its symbolic grapes to illustrate the jacket of this book. It has watched over Dutruch's comings and goings for over a hundred years.

Very concentrated and sometimes austere, the wine of Dutruch Grand Poujeaux is rather lacking in charm when it is young. Of all its neighbours, it seems to be the one to suffer most from growing pains. On the other hand, it is always very successful in off-years. "Its high tannin content makes it rather like the wines of Pauillac," says François Cordonnier, and he is not wrong. You have to wait several years to find the quintessence of Moulis wines from any Grand-Poujeaux. This was true of the fairly successful, well concentrated 75s, which took nearly ten years to develop, or "se faire" as the wine jargon would have it. This was also the case for the complex 79s and 81s, which were severe at first and took quite some time to bloon. Truly, Dutruch is a reliable old name which does honour to Moulis; in some years it definitely ranks among the best in the appellation. The quality of the last few vintages is the proof.

Fonréaud (Château)

Cru bourgeois

Commune: Listrac-Médoc. **Proprietor:** SCI Château Fonréaud (Chanfreau heirs). Manager: Jean Chanfreau. Vineyard manager: M. Lesca. Director: Marc Lalande. Cellar master: Paul Valverde. Consultant oenologist: Jacques Boissenot, Lamarque. **Size of vineyard:** 39 hectares. **Average age of vines:** 27 years. **Varieties:** 49% cabernet-sauvignon, 17% cabernet-franc, 31% merlot, 3% petit-verdot. **Production:** 200 *tonneaux,* 150,000 bottles CB. **Visits:** Monday to Friday, from 8 a.m. to noon and 2 to 5.30 p.m. Tel. 56 58 02 43. **Direct sales and by mail order:** in France. Château Fonréaud, Listrac-Médoc, 33480 Castelnau-de-Médoc. **Marketing:** now widely distributed through the Bordeaux trade.

Fonréaud, a fine mansion crowned by its lantern.

At one time Fonréaud was written Font Réaux, meaning Royal Fountain. And indeed, according to legend, the King of England is said to have stayed here in the eleventh century after finding a spring and a small pool. Of course there is nothing to prove this, but why should we doubt it? On the other hand it is beyond doubt that Fonréaud is a very old property, inhabited by the Duranteau family in the eighteenth century. After the Revolution, in 1791, it was bought by two brothers, Isaac and Guillaume d'Egmont, merchants on the Quai des Chartrons in Bordeaux. Eight years later, Isaac d'Egmont sold his share to his two nephews, Guillaume and Isaac von Hemert, who as well as having the same Christian names as their uncles were also merchants on the Quai des Chartrons. One of them was also the Danish consul in Bordeaux.

At the beginning of the nineteenth century, after divisions and inheritances, Alexandre de Bethmann became a member of the consortium of inheritors, then sold his half-share to his cousins. Finally, in 1832, François de Labeyrie bought Fonréaud for 100,000 francs. Chevalier de Saint-Louis, Baron de Savignac, and Colonel of the Guards, the new proprietor already owned estates in Bazas, Cudos, Maillas, Port-Sainte-Marie and Aillas, not to mention those owned by his wife, née Marie-Henriette de Mont d'Uzer de Lansac. In 1836 their only daughter Josephine married, giving Fonréaud to Clément Hyppolite Le Blanc de Mauvezin as her dowry. Their eldest son Henri had the château of today built with the stones from the little church in nearby Bouqueyran, which had been sequestered and sold under the Revolution. Built to plans by the architect Garros, the château is an elegant dwelling, surmounted by a bell-turret with two entirely different façades. Fonréaud remained in the Mauvezin family until 1958, when one of the descendants, the Vicomtesse de Coulogne, sold it for 160,000 francs to four lovers of Bordeaux wines, Messieurs Chambarière, Pierre and Edouard Castéja and Jacques Debayle. Four years later, Monsieur Léo Chanfreau, just returned from Algeria, became the majority shareholder in Fonréaud and later complete owner in 1964. Today his grandson Jean is in charge of this fine estate, largely replanted and restored over the last few years.

As in the time of the King of England, the little pool and the stream called Le Caput are still there. As for the little hill at Fonréaud, it is called Puy-de-Menjon and, at 43 metres, is recognized as the highest point in the Médoc. Its vineyard shares this privileged high position with its neighbour, Lestage, which also belongs to the Chanfreau family. But there are also several parcels on the other side of the road over towards Sémeillan, on the plateau of Carassonnat. The whole of the property and particularly the buildings have been the subject of an extensive renovation programme for some time, for Jean Chanfreau, the young vice-president of Listrac's Viticultural Federation, devotes himself wholeheartedly, to his vineyards and as a result the quality of the wine, which has had its ups and downs over the course of its long history, has now stabilized at a very high level. The 82, 83 and 85 vintages were highly successful; the 86 and 87 are just about ready for drinking now; they are well-balanced, well-rounded and have a rather long finish. But the most exciting of all is the 88, with its fine nose of cherry, and a firm, full attack; in the mouth it is wonderfully balanced. It is an excellent wine. The 89 too has a fine, well-balanced structure but, like the 87, it will undoubtedly be ready for drinking earlier than the excellent 88.

It is common practice to compare Lestage and Fonréaud because they are immediate neighbours, have the same soil and the same vintner. But I do not think this comparison is appropriate. Fonréaud's wine has its own personality and I find it better than that of its neighbour, having more grace, elegance and complexity. Lestage is undoubtedly more sturdily structured and more typical of Listrac. I prefer Fonréaud for its charm and smoothness. This *cru* is now well distributed through the Gironde wine trade and has made a successful comeback. Every spring it attracts its share of attention in the *primeurs* campaign of the *grands crus*.

Fontaine-Royale (Château) 🍷 → Fonréaud

Fourcas (Clos du)

Commune: Listrac-Médoc. **Proprietor:** Alain Miquau, Le Fourcas, Listrac-Médoc, 33480 Castelnau-de-Médoc. Tel. 56 58 01 63. Managed by: GAEC Lescoutra-Miquau. **Size of vineyard:** 12 hectares. **Average age of vines:** 15 years. **Varieties:** 33% cabernet-sauvignon, 65% merlot, 2% petit-verdot. **Production:** 50 tonneaux, 60,000 bottles CB. **Marketing:** vinification at Listrac's Cave Coopérative, tel. 56 58 03 19.

"In the eighteenth century, ploughing between the vine-rows in the Languedoc was done with a light swing-plough, called a 'fourcat', with an iron share," Fernand Braudel tells us in his remarkable book, *The Identity of France*. From the Languedoc to the Médoc, there is only one language, that of "Oc", and the name of the hamlet of Fourcas could well have its origins in the name of this ancient plough. Or else the lime kilns, the *fours à chaux* once numerous in the region, might have been responsible for the name after undergoing a phonetic change. However this may be, there is a Fourcas Hosten, a Fourcas Dupré and a Fourcas-Loubaney, so it is not surprising that there should be a Fourcas with no other adjunct. But this Fourcas is slightly different from the others, firstly because it is called a "Clos", and secondly because its wine is vinified at the *coopérative*. Since 1983, the estate has been run by Alain Miquau and Jean-Jacques Lescoutra, the sons, grandsons and great-grandsons of Listrac growers. But it belonged for a long time to the Miquau family, and Adrien, the grandfather, took his first harvest to the *coopérative* way back in 1935. There are several parcels of land, mainly on the gravelly soil of Le Tris and Le Fourcas, which are some of the best in the commune. The enthusiasm of these growers augurs well for the wines they produce. The magnum of Clos du Fourcas 79 was and still remains one of the best bottles of the *cave coopérative* of Listrac.

Fourcas Dupré (Château)

Commune: Listrac-Médoc. **Proprietor:** SC Château Fourcas Dupré. Manager: Patrice Pagès. Vineyard manager: Robert Creuzin. Cellar master: Alain Bouscarrut. Consultant oenologist: Jacques Boissenot, Lamarque. **Size of vineyard:** 40 hectares. **Average age of vines:** 25 years. **Varieties:** 50% cabernet-sauvignon, 10% cabernet-franc, 38% merlot, 2% petit-verdot. **Production:** 200 *tonneaux,* 250,000 bottles CB. **Visits:** Monday to Friday, from 8 a.m. to noon and 2 to 6 p.m. Tel. 56 58 01 07. **Direct sales and by mail order:** in France. Château Fourcas Dupré, Listrac-Médoc, 33480 Castelnau-de-Médoc. **Marketing:** sold direct for export and by representatives in France.

The little locality called Le Fourcas has been well known in the Médoc for many years for two reasons. Firstly, because it is one of the highest points in the area, and secondly because this altitude has been favourable to vine-growing from time immemorial. Belleyme's famous map, drawn up during the reign of Louis XV, in the eighteenth century bears witness to this. It is a plateau made up of one of the village's finest subsoils of gravel from the Pyrénées and the cabernet vines which grow there give excellent wine.

As is the case with Château Saransot-Dupré (see below), the property owes its name to Adolphe Dupré from Bordeaux, who bought it in 1843. He kept the vineyard for some thirty years, and his heirs sold it after his death. Then Fourcas Dupré passed through the hands of several different owners, among whom were well-known families in the viticultural world of Gironde – Raymond, Cathala, Dubos, Peyrelongue and others. When the Saint-Julien growers Paul and Michel Delon bought it in 1967, the estate was in a critical state. They put in hand a huge renovation programme lasting three years, restoring both buildings and the vineyard, which was sadly in need of attention. At the end of 1970 it was a much better estate that the Delons sold to the Pagès family and their partners. Fourcas Dupré had taken on a new lease of life thanks to the Delons, who vinified two harvests in their cellars at Château Léoville-Las Cases, but Guy Pagès also played a decisive role in its

Fourcas Dupré, vineyard and garden laid out in lines as straight as a die.

progress. Originally from the Languedoc region in the South of France, but long established in Tunisia, Guy Pagès was a thoroughly accomplished grower. He arrived in Listrac with the background of a grower who had been a pioneer in the vineyards of Tunisia and who had carried out extensive research, particularly in selecting clones. Under his care, the area under vine increased from 13 to 40 hectares within fifteen years. The *cru* of Bellevue-Laffont, also spelt Bellevue-Lafon and formerly vinified at the *cave coopérative*, was integrated with Fourcas. Its name now serves as a second label. Guy Pagès gave his property a new soul and buildings worthy of it. They can be seen on the way out of Listrac, on the right-hand side of the road to Saint-Laurent, and are open for visiting and direct sales. A promoter of first-class viticulture, independent and a stout defender of his appellation, Guy Pagès did more than simply adapt himself to his new territory: he brought along his experience, his confidence in the future and his abilities as a builder. His memory, like that of Pierre Saintout, another outstanding man from Listrac, and the former mayor Henri Bibian, is still very much alive in this commune on which he so firmly left his mark.

When he died in March 1985, his thirty-year-old son Patrice took up the reins. A director of the limited company which owns the estate, he is also in charge of vinification with the oenologist Jacques Boissenot. Breeding will out. Like his uncles who are also growers, one in the north of the Médoc at La Tour de By and the other at Berson in the Côtes de Blaye, Patrice Pagès produces a high class Listrac wine every year. With a hundred years' worth of medals, the wine of Fourcas Dupré is also successful in off-years such as 1980 or 1984. In great years it has a concentration, power and tannin which could allow it to be mistaken for a *cru classé* at blind tastings. Moreover, a preponderance of cabernet and one year's ageing in wood after a long fermentation period guarantee it a remarkably long life. It is clear that after a temporary eclipse in its fortunes, Fourcas Dupré has regained the excellent position it held, at the beginning of the century, for example, when its wines were sold at the same price as the best Pauillacs. Successively a *cru bourgeois supérieur,* then a *bourgeois exceptionnel*, it is now worthy of Féret's well-chosen words: "produces a wine of great merit". The description is apposite for Fourcas Dupré owes everything to merit and nothing to chance. If you want to place a bet on a Listrac wine do not forget this favourite. It may be rather slow at the start but always comes in among the winners at the finish, even after the longest of races.

Fourcas Hosten (Château)

Commune: Listrac-Médoc. **Proprietor:** SC du Château Fourcas Hosten. Managers: Bertrand de Rivoyre and Patrice Pagès. Estate manager: Bernard Coucharrière. Director and consultant oenologist: Claude Barthe. Cellar master: Claude Bibeyran. **Size of vineyard:** 46 hectares. **Average age of vines:** 20 years. **Varieties:** 50% cabernet-sauvignon, 40% merlot, 10% petit-verdot. **Production:** 200 *tonneaux*, 240,000 bottles CB. **Visits:** from 8.30 to 11.30 a.m. and 2.30 to 5.30 p.m., 4.30 p.m. on Fridays. **Direct sales:** Château Fourcas Hosten, Listrac-Médoc, 33480 Castelnau-de-Médoc. Tel. 56 58 01 15. **Marketing:** Ets de Rivoyre et Diprovin, Ets Schroeder et Schÿler.

Let us pay due tribute to the very best of the Listracs. For many years Fourcas Hosten was one of the leading lights among the commune's vineyards, but recently it has raised itself to the very pinnacle, thanks to the joint efforts of a few talented men, the perfect matching of grape varieties and terrain, and rigorous selection. The *cru* owes its name to the little locality where the vines grow, Le Fourcas, and to the fact that a Monsieur Hosten was owner of the estate in the nineteenth century. It was he who sold the land in 1810 to the Saint-Affrique family, who retained the property until 1971, when it was bought by a limited company headed by Monsieur Bertrand de Rivoyre.

Son of the broker Paul de Rivoyre, one of the most important personalities of his time in the Bordeaux wine world, Bertrand de Rivoyre arrived at Fourcas Hosten not just as a merchant but also as proprietor as he already was in the Côtes de Bourg (Château Guerry) and the Côtes de Castillon. On his new estate he found three vintages in the cellars, the 69s, 70s and 71s, representing a considerable stock; but he also found a completely dilapidated vat-house and working buildings needing numerous repairs. Working capital from a number of American shareholders helped to finance the reconstruction work, and Professor Emile Peynaud oversaw the vinification. The result of all this was not long in making itself felt and Fourcas Hosten produced an absolutely remarkable 73. At a blind tasting it was placed higher than many *crus classés*, a fact which was widely reported in the wine press. Since then it has given exceptionally consistent wines, even in off-years, as the seven gold medals won at Paris agricultural shows over ten years go to show. Since 1984 there has been a slight change in the firm's structure, for several American shareholders have sold their holdings, so enabling newcomers to take their place. Notable among there are the Pagès family from neighbouring Fourcas Dupré and Jean-Henry Schÿler, of Schroder & Schÿler, the well-known merchants.

The wine of Fourcas Hosten ages in the shadow of Listrac's church.

Fourcas Hosten's land is divided into two quite separate parcels. The larger is composed of gravel from the Pyrénées, so poor that not even lucerne will grow there. By contrast cabernet vines, with their roots which delve five metres down, grow wonderfully well. The other parcel, nearer the château, has soil of clayey limestone and is planted with merlot. It has a charming little country house built at the beginning of the last century, which looks out on to an attractive park on the garden side and at the back on to the delightful little church of Listrac, the mere width of a street away. The wine of Château Fourcas Hosten is only lightly filtered and ages for eighteen months in a cellar of eight hundred *barriques*. Some are new but the majority come from Château La Lagune, which boosts the quality. In addition, Bertrand de Rivoyre and his assistant Claude Barthe are rigorously selective when the time comes for blending, never hesitating to declassify the part of the production that they find least satisfactory, which is put out under a generic label.

In my humble opinion, the quality of Fourcas Hosten is always consistent, better than the *crus bourgeois* and, if ever the famous classification of 1855 were to be reviewed, it would deserve to be classified. Not only is it very representative of its appellation, but it has an elegance, even a distinction, which is rarely found in the wines of its leading neighbours. The 82 and 78 vintages, deep and complex, both powerful and elegant, are excellent examples of harmonious concentration and wonderful delicacy of bouquet. But this splendid wine should be given time to develop. The same is the case with the 83, 85 and the highly promising 89 vintages, whose bouquet and charm guarantee a great wine. The astonishingly high quality of the Fourcas Hosten 87 should be mentioned too, with its aromas of coffee, discreetly woody, and a delicacy wholly unexpected from this vintage.

Fourcas-Loubaney (Château)

Cru bourgeois

Commune: Listrac-Médoc. **Proprietor:** S.E.A. du Château Listrac. *Vineyard manager:* Franck Hostens. **Size of vineyard:** 4 hectares. **Average age of vines:** 35 years. **Varieties:** 60% cabernet-sauvignon, 40% merlot. **Production:** 20 *tonneaux,* 20,000 bottles CB. **Visits:** Monday to Friday from 8 a.m. to 6 p.m.; by appointment at weekends and for groups of more than 20 people; for information, tel. 56 58 03 83. **Direct sales and by mail order:** in France. Château Moulin de Laborde, Listrac-Médoc, 33480 Castelnau-de-Médoc. **Marketing:** 50% export, 30% retail, 20% to private clients.

In 1977 Michel Hostens (see Moulin de Laborde) bought the four hectares which remained of the very old *cru of* Loubaney, on the gravelly plateau of Fourcas. This little vineyard had existed since the beginning of the nineteenth century and Loubaneys had followed in each other's footsteps for many decades.

This acquisition has enabled Hostens, an astute grower, to market a sort of *tête de cuvée,* readily distinguished from the Moulin de Laborde, where the wine was actually vinified. Then in 1989 he sold the two estates to the Novalliance Group, a Paris firm whose president, Alain Mallard, also bought Château Listrac and La Bécade. Formely a banker and now a businessman specializing in packaging, logistics and transportation, Alain Mallard today owns nearly 60 hectares of vines in Listrac as a result of his various acquisitions all over the appellation. One of these is Château Listrac, a little château built in the nineteenth century, standing at the entrance to the village. He at once renovated all the buildings to have rooms for receiving and accommodating visitors, and for tastings. A library specializing in works concerning wine has just been installed. Various *crus* from the Listrac appellation can be bought here too.

Franquet Grand Poujeaux (Château)

Cru bourgeois

Commune: Moulis-en-Médoc. **Proprietor:** Pierre Lambert. **Director:** Jean-Michel Lambert. **Size of vineyard:** 7 hectares. **Average age of vines:** 20 years. **Varieties:** 35% cabernet-sauvignon, 25% cabernet-franc, 30% merlot, 2% malbec, 8% petit-verdot. **Production:** 30 *tonneaux,* 35,000 bottles CB. **Visits:** Monday to Friday from 2 to 7 p.m. but preferably by appointment, Jean-Michel Lambert, tel. 56 59 04 94. **Direct sales and by mail order:** in France. Château Franquet Grand Poujeaux, 6, rue des Lilas, 33250 Pauillac. **Marketing:** in France, sales direct to dealers; abroad, sales to direct importers.

The Franquets were growers at Grand Poujeaux in the nineteenth century. At the beginning of the twentieth their vineyard, which had come into the possession of the Lambert family, took the name of Cru Robert-Franquet, and more recently it became Franquet Grand Poujeaux. So the name encompasses the double nature of its origin, human and geographical. Run by Pierre Lambert and his son Jean-Michel, this little estate is a model of family and growing tradition. Like good Médocains, they cultivate five different varieties, some on the gravel ridges, others on the slopes of clayey limestone. "Together these two different types of land give our wine its essential qualities," the Lamberts say. "While the poor, permeable Quaternary gravel gives it vivacity, brilliance, finesse and delicacy, the clayey limestone provides body, substance and tannin. All these qualities go together to make a generous wine which develops slowly. It reaches its peak after about six to ten years."

All this sums up the situation perfectly. The Lamberts also give good advice on the best way to drink their wine: "Swirl it in your glass, hold it up to the light, inhale deeply, and sip slowly. And what to accompany it with? It depends on the vintage. A young full-bodied wine with red meats, rich stews, game and cep mushrooms; an old or lighter wine with grilled meats and fish, white meat and desserts. Never anything containing vinegar. Serve the wine neither too warm nor too cold: the ideal temperature is around 14° -16° C (57° -60° F)." I have nothing to add to the suggestions of these conscientious growers, except that in my humble opinion you can drink a good Moulis at 18° C (64° F), but that is a matter of taste. Their wine benefits from a long fermentation period (nearly a month), clears in the vat during winter and is bottled only after ageing for two years. It is sound wine made in the old-fashioned way which you can hand down to your grandchildren. As such, this relatively unknown *cru* symbolizes fairly well the authentic viticultural traditions of the Médoc. Although a bit overshadowed by the media awareness and international prestige of larger labels, this school of thought still has its faithful supporters. This ancestral know-how has proved itself well, and owes nothing to current fashion.

Gobinaud (Château)

Commune: Listrac-Médoc. **Proprietor:** the Gobinaud brothers. Managers, estate and vineyard managers: Gobinaud Frères et Fils. Consultant oenologist: Pierre Bariteau, Castelnau. **Size of vineyard:** 8 hectares. **Average age of vines:** 30 years. **Varieties:** 40% cabernet-sauvignon, 10% cabernet-franc, 40% merlot, 2% malbec, 8% petit-verdot. **Production:** 45 *tonneaux*, 30,000 bottles CB. **Visits:** Monday to Friday, by appointment. Jean or Yves Gobinaud, tel. 56 58 03 36 or 56 58 02 15. **Direct sales and by mail order:** in France and abroad. Château Gobinaud, Lafon, Listrac-Médoc, 33480 Castelnau-de-Médoc. **Marketing:** through Bordeaux.

Since the beginning of the nineteenth century, the Gobinauds have been growers on the plateau of Les Marcieux between Peyrelebade and Lafon where, it is said, there was once a dolmen. Neither wars nor crises, frost (though it was fatal in 1985), mildew or hail have interrupted this vine-growing family's life here, firmly rooted in the soil of Listrac. So it comes as no surprise to learn that grandfather Gobinaud won a silver medal in Brussels in 1876 for a bottle whose label (today reverently preserved) carried only three lines: Cru Gobinaud – Graves de Lafon – Listrac Médoc. It is no more surprising that on October 30, 1902, the offices of the Bordeaux *négociant* Dagnial & Co bought, through the broker Dubois, eighty *barriques* of the 1901 "at the price of 275 francs in Bordeaux *barriques* of its year, correctly measured, full after topping up to compensate for ullage", according to the invoice, duly signed, countersigned and initialled.

Close to the forest, but protected from frost, this parcel enjoys its own microclimate.

Today the brothers Yves and Jean Gobinaud, with their son and nephew Jean-François, cultivate this family vineyard, on typical soil of clayey limestone with a good north to south exposure. The huge stones thrown up from the ground during ploughing have served to build entire barns in the neighbourhood. From time to time fossils come to light. For thirty-five years, the whole of Gobinaud's production was automatically bought up by the *négociant* firm of Borie. Then the Gobinaud brothers began to develop a private clientele themselves, either by selling direct at the property or from stands at the markets and fairs all over the south-west of France. They are often to be seen in the Dordogne and in the Landes, at Soulac and at Font-Romeu. This itinerant marketing works. It is not uncommon for Jean Gobinaud to sell fifty cases in one weekend and return home with an empty van. It is true that it is difficult to resist the charm of this man who is physically rather similar to his wine – warm, stimulating and ruddy. He is also a formidable actor, as he demonstrates at the annual festival celebrating the "vin nouveau" organized by Listrac's Viticultural Federation. He generally appears disguised as Bacchus astride a cask carried by his colleagues, in a toga and wearing a laurel wreath, splendid as a Greek god. The face of this honest grower, glowing and pink faced after the dinner he has just finished, lights up even more when everybody joins in singing the local hymn:

> "Joyous colleagues who love our peninsula dear,
> My soul chagrin ne'er shall betide.
> When I feel my face redden and glowing with cheer,
> My native Médoc is my pride."

Encore after encore follows, just like the glasses of wine drunk before the song. The Gobinauds, mercifully free of faddism and intellectual pretensions, maintain the tradition of a region which knows how to celebrate. It is not surprising that their wine shares some of their characteristics. Powerful, tannic, generous, it is clearly vinified in the old way, fined twice with egg-white and remains for two years in wood. It needs time to open up but its robust constitution is a guarantee of a long

126

and happy life – both for itself and for those who drink it. Gobinaud 61 is the living proof of this wine's great ageing potential. I discovered this magnificent bottle in 1990 with friends who, in an informal blind tasting, mistook it for a *cru classé*. At nearly thirty years of age, this wine was still very young and vigorous. It made us feel just the same and quite eager to repeat the experience with later vintages.

Grand Listrac (Cave coopérative)

Commune: Listrac-Médoc. **Proprietor:** Cave de vinification des Grands Vins de Listrac. President: Maurice Meyre. Vice-Presidents: David Raymond and Alain Miquau. Cellar master: André Seubes. Consultant oenologist: M. Perez. **Size of vineyard:** 170 hectares. **Average age of vines:** 25 years. **Varieties:** 30% cabernet-sauvignon, 60% merlot, 2% malbec, 8% petit-verdot. **Production:** 800 *tonneaux,* 400,000 bottles CB. **Visits:** daily from 9 a.m. to noon and 2 to 5.30 p.m. M. Cassegrain, tel. 56 58 03 19. **Direct sales and by mail order:** in France. Cave de vinification de Listrac, Listrac-Médoc, 33480 Castelnau-de-Médoc. **Marketing:** 15% to the trade and 20% to distributors and restaurants.

We are in Paris and the year is 1948. Quite by chance, Georges Chagniat, chief buyer for the Compagnie des Wagons-lits, is drinking a bottle labelled Grand Listrac 1945 in the company of a friend. In a moment of destiny, Chagniat falls in love with this previously unknown wine. But at that time it was not enough just to drink a bottle in order to claim to know a wine. Motivated by professional conscientiousness, he decides to discover its source and takes the train as far as Moulis-Listrac station. He gets out in torrential rain, opens his umbrella and, in order to ask the way, knocks at the door of the first house he comes to. "Ah, there you are at last!", a complete stranger says to him on the doorstep, impatiently awaiting the arrival of the vet to treat his horse. Chagniat apologizes and explains that he is not very well up in equine medicine, but is looking for the *coopérative*. He finally arrives and finds there Monsieur Sauts, the treasurer, and Pierre Saintout, the father-in-law of the future president of Listrac's Viticultural Federation, as well as Monsieur Thibaut, the secretary. With them Chagniat carefully tastes once again the famous 45, finds it even better and on the spot orders thirty *tonneaux* – one hundred and twenty casks, or 270 hectolitres, for consumption by the SNCF's travellers in its dining-cars.

This story is entirely true and is the starting point of the extraordinary union between Listrac and the railways. For from 1948 onwards, the railway company bought Grand Listrac every year, ordering as much as 1,500 hectolitres (a third of the production) by the end of the sixties. The wine featured on the dining-cars' wine list beside with Pontet Canet, Bourgogne and Côtes-du-Rhône. "The SNCF had not then invented its 'self-service' dining-cars with their pallid chips, washed down with those Beaujolais wines which, through they have been chaptalized, are so disheartening," as Jean-Paul Kauffman wrote so rightly in a delightful article in *L'Amateur de Bordeaux.* Thus it was that every year, once the preceding year's verbal contract had been tacitly renewed, the wine left the *cave coopérative* in special tankers destined for Saint-Ouen, where the railway company had its cellars. There it aged for eighteen months in the famous undated 36 cl half-bottles before being offered to travellers. However great the trade's disappointment may have been at failing to corner this worthwhile market, it should be acknowledged that these half-bottles did 127

An ultra-modern vat-house for a truly "grand" Listrac.

more to publicize Listrac than all the festivals, wine-brotherhoods and other tastings of the century put together. "I met Monsieur Chagniat several times," relates Maurice Meyre, the current president of the *coopérative*. "He was a charming man, a refined taster but demanding. He came to taste the wine every spring for some twenty years. The railways made Listrac known just when it needed of publicity and it is thanks to them that we were recognized as a communal appellation in 1957. The growers of Listrac have the *cave* to thank for that."

Today, however, Grand Listrac is no longer a leading light in railway gastronomy. The SCNF has extended its wine list to include other regions, notably Saint-Emilion, and now orders no more than 400 hectolitres per year, sufficient for the name still to feature after forty years of loyal and sterling service – a fine example of fidelity. As for the *coopérative* itself, it celebrated its fiftieth anniversary in September 1985, inaugurating at the same time a superb new vat-house and considerable new extensions. Like nearly all the other *coopératives,* the Listrac *coopérative* was born as a result of the terrible depression between the two world wars. In 1934 twenty or so growers in Listrac, realizing that they were heading for ruin, started to think of joining together in order to weather the storm. With the advice of Jean-Charles Cazes, whose personality will long be remembered in Pauillac, and of Monsieur

Villepigue, the first president of the Federation of the Gironde *Caves*, they established a *coopérative* for vinification.

After several meetings, nine representatives of vineyards facing threat found themselves in front of Monsieur Figerou, a notary in Castelnau, on May 23, 1935 and signed the birth certificate of Listrac's *coopérative*, the fifth in the Médoc. They started out twenty-five-strong but, with a steady stream of new members, they have now grown to three times that number. The number of members has never stopped increasing and even takes in several small proprietors in Moulis. In 1986, the *cave* represented 160 hectares of vines, with varieties in the approximate proportions of 60% merlot, 30% cabernet and 10% petit-verdot and malbec.

With a picture of a proud sailing-ship on its label, Grand Listrac is the principal brand name. But the *cave coopérative* also makes other wines under names such as Château Guitignan from Moulis and the wines of Moulin du Bourg, Château Capdet, Clos du Fourcas and Vieux Moulin, Listrac estates which have retained their own label. It also makes and finally a generic Moulis from some five or so hectares of vines in that commune, sold in bulk. Marketing is principally by direct sales and private customers. A computerized file lists 20,000 clients throughout France, mostly in the Paris region, the north and the east. Tourists can call every day (except for the major religious holidays) and they will be warmly welcomed with a tour and tasting, and may buy direct. Sales have now risen to 400,000 bottles per annum and the stock of nearly one million bottles includes the excellent 78, 79 and 82 vintages. In sum, Grand Listrac represents good value for money and certain bottles are the equals of château wines costing twice as much. It is generally well placed in blind tastings and it has all the good qualities of Listrac wine – power, long life and virility.

Granins Grand Poujeaux (Château)

Commune: Moulis-en-Médoc. **Proprietor:** André Batailley. **Size of vineyard:** 6 hectares. **Average age of vines:** 20 years. **Varieties:** 35% cabernet-sauvignon, 50% merlot, 5% malbec, 10% petit-verdot. **Production:** 30 *tonneaux,* 20,000 bottles CB. **Direct sales and by mail order:** in France. Monsieur André Batailley, Grand-Poujeaux, Moulis-en-Médoc, 33480 Castelnau-de-Médoc. Tel. 56 58 02 99.

Victor-Edouard Batailley, born in 1902 in Vertheuil and still as fit as ever despite his considerable age, is one of the oldest figures in the little growing world of

Grand-Poujeaux. A professional nurseryman, he settled there on January 1, 1928 and replanted Chasse-Spleen's vineyard, which at that time was made up of vines which were too old. From 1934 he began to buy small parcels of uncultivated land which he planted for himself. Today retired, but awarded the Mérite Agricole medal, Monsieur Batailley has divided his estate between his son André and his son-in-law Jean-Louis Telley. Two-thirds of the vineyard is situated next to Maucaillou on fine gravel, typical of the terrain of Grand-Poujeaux. The name of Granins already featured on the land register at the beginning of the century and, in 1922 Edouard Féret wrote: "Remarkably well kept, the estate produces fine, mellow wines, highly appreciated and sought after by wine merchants." Nearly seventy years later, this observation holds true.

Grave Richebon (Château)

Commune: Moulis-en-Médoc. **Proprietor:** Jacques Richebon. Consultant oenologist: Jacques Boissenot, Lamarque. **Size of vineyard:** 2.06 hectares. **Average age of vines:** 25 years. **Varieties:** 35% cabernet-sauvignon, 15% cabernet-franc, 35% merlot, 15% petit-verdot. **Production:** 10,000 bottles CB. **Direct sales and by mail order:** in France. Jacques Richebon, Petit-Poujeaux, Moulis-en-Médoc, 33480 Castelnau-de-Médoc. Tel. 56 58 18 70. **Marketing:** through the Bordeaux trade.

Jacques Richebon, born in the Médoc and proprietor of Château Grave Richebon since 1959, cultivates 2.6 hectares stretching from Grand-Poujeaux to Moulis. He is the son of a family of growers, and in 1964 won both the gold medal at the Regional Competition in Bordeaux and the silver medal at the Paris agricultural show. Since then, the quality of his wines has continued to improve. The 70 and 74 were excellent and the 81 remarkable. Delicate and with a deep colour, its bouquet is indefinably "special". Those who have been fortunate enough to taste it say it is well rounded and will age well.

Gressier Grand Poujeaux (Château)

Commune: Moulis-en-Médoc. **Proprietor:** Bernard de Saint-Affrique Heirs. Director and manager: Bertrand de Marcellus. Consultant oenologists: MM. Gendrot and Couasnon, Pauillac. **Size of vineyard:** 18 hectares. **Average age of vines:** 25 years. **Varieties:** 55% cabernet-sauvignon, 10% cabernet-franc, 35% merlot. **Production:** 80 *tonneaux,* 90,000 bottles CB. **Visits:** Monday to Friday from 8.30 to 11.30 a.m. and 2 to 5 p.m. **Direct sales and by mail order:** in France. Château Gressier Grand Poujeaux, Moulis-en-Médoc, 33480 Castelnau-de-Médoc. **Marketing:** 80% to the Bordeaux trade.

What do the three black heads on the label's emblem mean? That the wine has a flavour of cep mushrooms? True, in good years it has very pleasant aromas of the

Messieurs de Marcellus and de Saint-Affrique.

forest floor, but that is not the explanation. Unfortunately, we have to go back to the time of the ebony trade in which the Atlantic ports engaged under the Ancien Régime to discover the origin of this unexpected heraldry. At least, this is a possible source though far from certain, though it is a matter of historical fact that Bordeaux ship owners were involved in the slave trade, euphemistically called the "triangular trade". However, all this has little to do with the excellent *cru* of Gressier which owes its name to its creator Monsieur Gressier, who bought the property in 1760, making it one of the oldest vineyards in Moulis. Two hundred and thirty years later its owners changed their name, although it remained in the same family, for Mademoiselle Zamé Gressier married Alphonse de Saint-Affrique in 1850. Their direct descendant, Philippe de Saint-Affrique, has lived at Gressier for more than forty years and has produced astounding vintages. Today his grandson, Bertrand de Marcellus, is the estate's manager.

The long history of Gressier has had its ups and downs. In 1820 one of the Gressier daughters married, taking with her as dowry half of the vineyard, which became independent and was known for many years afterwards as Chasse-Spleen. At the end of the nineteenth century the dreaded phylloxera ravaged the Gironde and destroyed twenty hectares of Gressier's vines. Nearer our own time, an extraordinary July hailstorm destroyed the entire 1975 harvest. Finally, bowing to hard-hearted Mother Nature, the 1963, 65 and 77 vintages were not put in bottle, as they were not considered worthy of the château. This deliberate policy of selecting only the best was carried out for a long time by Baron Philippe de Saint-Affrique, owner of the excellent *cru* Fourcas Hosten in Listrac until 1971. He raised his two wines to the highest standard of their appellation and, although they were both vinified at Gressier, each retained its individuality. He has now retired but both wines still bear his stamp in the shape of an untarnished reputation – and two labels so closely resembling each other that they are easy to confuse.

Gressier owes its quality to several important factors: its land is 90% pure Garonne gravel on the ridge of Grand-Poujeaux, and its dominant proportion of cabernet gives elegance and long life. Deliberately restricted yields, the result of traditional methods, give an intense concentration of tannin. Certain parcels, planted with very old vines, do not yield more than fifteen hectolitres per hectare. Lastly, pruning stops at two buds and a rigorous thinning out of the leaves helps each plant to give its best. As to vinification, it should be noted that when the Médoc was installing stainless steel vats everywhere, Comte de Marcellus equipped his vat-house with huge oval casks of oak, so continuing a serious, long-standing tradition. But all these factors together do not make a wine that can be drunk immediately. In the last decade, Gressier has been particularly successful with the 82 and 83 vintages and the astonishing 84 is certainly one of the best in the appellation. More recent vintages should be kept in the cellar in order to appreciate them at their best. But lovers of young wines will find that they have an entirely consistent quality. On the other hand, the 24s, 26s 28s and 29s, religiously preserved at the château (as are bottles of the 1887), reveal an amazing power and an exceptional charm.

Gressier has always been among the leaders of Moulis. In years when expertise was all important (55,73,76), it achieved a standard equivalent to a very good *cru classé*. It has the skill to maintain this position with ease, but also with the unassuming sincerity befitting any long and exacting labour. It must be said that Gressier chose a long time ago to market its wine primarily through the Bordeaux trade and as a result is one of the most renowned wines of Moulis, and one of the most well distributed for export. The market now counts on this *cru's* regularity and seriousness to respond to the fairly strong demand from Benelux and the United Kingdom, a demand for the *crus bourgeois* of the Médoc which doesn't cease to grow.

Guitignan (Château)

Commune: Moulis-en-Médoc. **Proprietor:** Monsieur Marc Lestage. **Size of vineyard:** 6 hectares. **Average age of vines:** 30 years. **Varieties:** 40% cabernet-franc, 60% merlot. **Production:** 100 hectolitres approximately, 13,000 bottles CB. **Marketing:** vinification at Listrac's *cave coopérative*. tel. 56 58 03 19.

Although it is vinified and marketed by Listrac's *cave coopérative*, and reduced to 6 hectares, Château Guitignan keeps one of the oldest Moulis names alive. The Lestage family has been its owners since the seventeenth century, and before the First World War their wine sold dearer than the *bourgeois supérieurs* because of its high quality and long-standing reputation. Today, Guitignan no longer enjoys its former fame but, with yields which are deliberately kept at a low level and a combination of varieties unique in the appellation (cabernet-franc and merlot), it remains perfectly worthy of interest, as can be seen from the excellent 83. Light, elegant and with a delicate bouquet, it is a wine which does not need to wait ten years to be ready, and it has the advantage of being reasonably priced. Château Guitignan is a lovely family mansion located at Le Bourdieu.

Haut Brugas (Domaine du)

Commune: Listrac-Médoc. **Proprietor:** Charlotte Bispalie. Run by: Monsieur Pierre Bispalie. **Size of vineyard:** 3 hectares. **Average age of vines:** 15 to 20 years. **Varieties:** 50% cabernet-sauvignon, 50% merlot. **Production:** 10,000 bottles CB. **Visits:** daily, by appointment, tel. 56 58 03 13. **Direct sales:** Domaine du Haut Brugas, Médrac, Listrac-Médoc, 33480 Castelnau-de-Médoc. **Marketing:** sales to individual customers.

A discreet blue sign at the crossroads of two paths in the proprietor's kitchen garden announces to passers-by that Haut Brugas sells direct to the public. The late Charles Bispalie lived here from 1951 and today it is his wife who owns this little vineyard, solidly planted in the fine gravel of Médrac. Because of its geology, this Listrac hamlet, neighbouring the best land in Moulis, is an important growing site in the Médoc, particularly because it is the only plateau in Listrac to have authentic Quaternary Gunz gravel, containing silex, quartz, agglomerates, ferruginous sandstone, agates and so forth.

At an altitude of twenty-six metres on the most westerly part of the Listrac appellation, Château Haut Brugas maintains the tradition of the *crus artisans*, but in a princely soil. Visitors will be warmly welcomed – even more so if you have taken the time to make an appointment – and can be sure of finding bottles of good wine, modestly priced, and a choice of several vintages.

Haut-Plantey (Château)

Commune: Listrac-Médoc. **Proprietor:** Louis Rami. **Size of vineyard:** 1.73 hectares. **Average age of vines:** 25 years. **Varieties:** 25% cabernet-sauvignon, 50% merlot, 25% petit-verdot. **Production:** 2,500 bottles CB. **Visits:** possible. **Direct sales:** Château Haut-Plantey, Louis Rami, Lafon, Listrac-Médoc, 33480 Castelnau-de-Médoc. **Marketing:** M. Fremiaud, at Le Bouscat, and dealers in Belgium (planned).

You think you will never get there! "Lafon" seems to be at the end of the world, buried in deepest Listrac, almost deserted and apparently uninhabited. And yet everything breathes wine here: row upon row of vines as far as the eye can see. It is worth seeking out Château Haut-Plantey and getting to know its likeable owner, Louis Rami, with his kindly face, in his early sixties and happy to live in the middle of his vines, alone or nearly so in this spot on which man has hardly made his mark. For him his wine is his life and, like his father, grandfather and great-grandfather before him, he devotes himself passionately to creating from his little vineyard a *cru* worthy of its appellation.

His methods are just as traditional as his devotion to his calling: meticulous care, true art. And Louis Rami's greatest joy is a pleasure which warms his heart – the satisfaction of making good wine.

Jordi (Château)

Commune: Moulis-en-Médoc. **Proprietor:** Guy Coubris. Vineyard manager: C. Frances. Cellar master: Robert Dupuy. Consultant oenologist: Pierre Bariteau, Castelnau. **Size of vineyard:** 3.57 hectares. **Average age of vines:** 40 years. **Varieties:** 25% cabernet-sauvignon, 73% merlot, 2% petit-verdot. **Production:** 15 *tonneaux,* 18,000 bottles CB. **Visits:** Guy Coubris, tel. 56 58 15 23. **Direct sales and by mail order:** in France and abroad. Château Jordi, Guy Coubris, 21, rue Victor-Hugo, 33480 Castelnau-de-Médoc. **Marketing:** direct to the United States and Canada through the château's agents.

Château Jordi is one of Moulis's most recent labels, with 4 hectares of vines, some more than sixty years old, scattered about in small parcels on very old vine-growing soi!. The property was created in 1984 by Guy Coubris, the former mayor of Castelnau, whose brother owns Château La Mouline. Jordi's wine ages in second-hand *barriques* bought from Château Latour. It is marked by the predominance of merlot which gives it a pleasant, velvety quality. The label, with its gold lettering on a black background, strongly resembles that of Château Palmer. No doubt Guy Coubris would like his wine to be compared to it too. Château Jordi is not yet very well known, but it can and should improve on the conditions that yields stay at a reasonable level and that the maturation of the grapes is given first priority.

La Bécade (Château)

Cru bourgeois

Commune: Listrac-Médoc. **Proprietor:** S.E.A. du Château Listrac. Vineyard manager: Monsieur François Xavier Gravellier. **Size of vineyard:** 21.75 hectares. **Average age of vines:** 20 years. **Varieties:** 58% cabernet-sauvignon, 42% merlot. **Production:** 125 *tonneaux,* 120,000 bottles CB. **Direct sales and by mail order:** in France. Château La Bécade, Listrac-Médoc, 33480 Castelnau-de-Médoc. Tel. 56 58 01 09 or 56 67 12 30. **Marketing:** through the Bordeaux trade.

It is well known that the woods around Listrac abound in game, and the name "La Bécade", formerly "La Bécasse" (woodcock), is an indication of this. This old estate has changed hands many times. In the nineteenth century it belonged to the Bethmann family, and in particular to Alexandre de Bethmann, mayor of Bordeaux from 1867 to 1870. Then it was bought by Félix Clauzel, a large landowner in the canton; but the wine went under the name of Château du Cartillon, a famous vineyard in Lamarque. Following this, a Monsieur Pautard from Lorraine owned the property, which his widow sold in 1935 to her cousin Désiré Cordier. Six years later the estate was bought by Monsieur Dencausse, an ironmonger at La Brède, who remained its owner until 1964. La Bécade then had the good fortune to fall into the hands of Jean-Pierre Théron, who had lived in Morocco and who completely reorganized the estate, then reduced to five hectares. After much hard work over the

La Bécade, now a splendid whole again.

years, including exchanging no fewer than eighty parcels, he established a vineyard of twenty hectares in one unbroken stretch around the house at Donissan. Finally Jean-Pierre Théron decided to sell La Bécade in 1990 to the Novalliance Group, which we encountered at Château Fourcas Loubaney. Despite their love of the Médoc, Jean-Pierre Théron and his wife (who is the mayor of Portets, in the Graves region) were no longer able to keep a tight rein on all their activities, whether on their wine-producing estates or in the wine fraternities, where they are particulary active.

The wine of La Bécade is not typical of the Listracs for it does not have the appellation's richness or usual fullness. Clearly marked by the cabernets on sandy soil and subsoil of clay, it is usually a supple wine. Aged exclusively in vats, it does not benefit from being in wood and takes no tannin from oak casks. The result is generally a rather round, well-balanced wine, which cannot be faulted, but which lacks personality. It has the advantage of being able to be drunk young, but it lacks vigour and intensity, qualities which are compensated for by its incontestable elegance. A few hectolitres from petits-verdots and some casks of new wood would certainly be an advantage, giving richer aromas and so being more attractive to the customer of today.

Laborde-Canterane (Château)

Like Château Bergeron, Laborde-Canterane represents another label for Philippe Dourthe, but the wine is from Duplessis-Fabre, and has all its qualities. It is very widely distributed to restaurants, particularly in Paris. Moreover Laborde-Canterane went down in the pages of history at the beginning of the 1980s, when it was served at the table of the EEC heads of government at a summit conference in Paris. This was the 1975 vintage, and it is said that Pierre Mauroy was so taken with it that he ordered several cases for his personal cellar. This label does not refer to an autonomous *cru,* but is rather a specific packaging for a wine known by other names. This takes nothing away from its qualities. *See Duplessis-Fabre.*

La Closerie du Grand-Poujeaux (Ch.)

Commune: Moulis-en-Médoc. **Proprietor:** GFA Le Grand-Poujeaux. **Manager:** Jeanne Bacquey. **Consultant oenologist:** CEIO Pauillac (M. Couasnon). **Size of vineyard:** 6 hectares. **Average age of vines:** 25 years. **Varieties:** 65% cabernet-sauvignon, 30% merlot, 5% petit-verdot. **Production:** 18 to 20 *tonneaux,* 20,000 bottles CB. **Direct sales and by mail order:** in France and abroad. Jeanne Bacquey, Grand-Poujeaux, Moulis-en-Médoc, 33480 Castelnau-de-Médoc. Tel. 56 58 01 89. **Marketing:** French merchants and foreign importers.

The Douats are one of the oldest vine-growing families in the canton, and the communes in the Haut-Médoc which have not known one of the heirs of this important dynasty at one time or another are few indeed. At the beginning of the century La Closerie belonged to Fernand Douat. The vineyard had been created by his father-in-law, Monsieur Segonnes, the former estate manager at Chasse-Spleen. Today it still belongs to Madame Douat but it is reduced to 4 hectares. In 1984 it was taken on by the Bacqueys (see Bel-Air Lagrave), in the form of a Groupement Foncier Agricole (GFA), which manages both properties together. The bonds linking the two families and the fact that the two vineyards lie side by side have helped to seal this union.

As managers of the estate the Bacqueys have started to replant several parcels which have been unproductive until now. The total land of the two estates will then come to about 25 hectares. At one time the wine of La Closerie was very popular in Holland, and for many years it was to be found on the tables of French ambassadors and consuls abroad. Its new management could well help to restore it to its former success.

Laffitte-Cantegric (Château)

Cantegric should not be confused with Cantegril, the name of a former mayor of Listrac who was also the owner of Château Clarke. It, along with several other similarly named parcels in the canton, owes its origins to an ancient name which translates "the place where the cricket sings". At the beginning of the century, this *cru* belonged to a grower with an equally evocative name – Léon Pommepy. Its fame was widespread, for it was mostly sold for export, particularly to Russia. Then the vineyard became attached to Château Pierre Bibian, for which it was a sort of second label (like Bibian-Darriet). When he bought Château Pierre Bibian, Jean Tigana, the great French footballer, immediately decided to restore the name Laffitte-Cantegric to its former glory. At this time he decided to reserve it for the property's best wine, after rigorous selection from the vats and casks, for which the footballer-grower called on the best advice. Thus Laffitte-Cantegric made its reappearance as a top quality wine with an official début in June 1987 in a much-promoted launch and tasting organized in Bordeaux by Listrac's Viticultural Federation. Samples of the 1986 vintage were particularly appreciated. And on the same day day Jean Tigana also scored an important goal in the deciding match of the league championship. However, some three years later the future of this label is unclear.

Lafon (Château)

Cru bourgeois

Commune: Listrac-Médoc. **Proprietor:** Monsieur Jean-Pierre Théron, Listrac-Médoc, 33480 Castelnau-de-Médoc. Tel. 56 58 01 13 or 56 67 12 30. Vineyard manager: Henri Meunier. **Size of vineyard:** 14.1 hectares. **Average age of vines:** 19 years. **Varieties:** 54% cabernet-sauvignon, 46% merlot. **Production:** 75 *tonneaux,* 70,000 bottles CB. **Marketing:** through Bordeaux.

Lafon is one of the hamlets furthest from the village of Listrac, next to the communes of Cussac and Lamarque, and however far we go back in time wine has always been made there: not round the houses, but on the nearby plateau of Les Marcieux. At the beginning of the century Dominique Douat, a remarkable wine maker, lent a certain prestige to Château Lafon, where he cultivated very old malbec vines which had withstood phylloxera. Twenty hectares of vines, some over a hundred years old, produced a wine which was judged to be exceptional, full bodied and deep in colour. But even in the nineteenth century Château Lafon had collected an impressive number of medals, as witnessed by the old diplomas hanging in their frames on the walls of the cellar, decorated with images that are now rather old-fashioned, but so elaborate, ornamental and beautifully written that they make a fine collection.

Jean-Pierre Théron, who already owned Château La Bécade, bought the neighbouring Lafon from Madame Catherine Boyé in 1969. From a very old family of growers, first in the *département* of Gard, then in Algeria, he modernized the property and made it more functional, with self-cooling stainless steel vats and an unusual installation for drying the grapes in case of rainy harvests, in order to obtain the deepest possible colour. The vineyard lies in one unbroken stretch on a subsoil of clayey marl, and the cellar doors can be recognized by their attractive wrought ironwork. The wine is vinified and aged in the same way as that of La Bécade, from which it differs only by its label. Its firmness and full-bodied personality are characteritic of the Listrac appellation.

Château Lafon's vat-house has no reason to envy the best equipped of Grands Crus.

Lagorce (Domaine de) 🍷 → *La Mouline*

La Grave de Guitignan (Château) 🍷

→ *Anthonic*

La Gravette (Château) 🍷 → *Reverdi*

La Gravière Grand Poujeaux (Ch.) 🍷

→ *Dutruch Grand Poujeaux*

Lalande (Château)   ♙♙♙♙♙

Cru bourgeois

Commune: Listrac-Médoc. **Proprietor:** Mme G. Darriet.
Size of vineyard: 10.7 hectares. **Average age of vines:**
25 years. **Varieties:** 40% cabernet-sauvignon, 50% merlot,
10% petit-verdot. **Production:** 50 *tonneaux,* 50,000 bottles
CB. **Visits:** daily from 8 a.m. to 7 p.m., Sundays by ap-
pointment. Tel. 56 58 19 45. **Direct sales and by mail order:**
Mme Darriet, Château Lalande, Listrac-Médoc, 33480
Castelnau-de-Médoc. **Marketing:** one third through the
Bordeaux trade.

The Duboscqs have been making wine at Château Lalande, a *cru bourgeois* of
long-standing fame, for more than a hundred years. The estate, one of the furthest
to the west of Listrac, situated on the sandy, forested side of the commune, actually
covers some 220 hectares. But the vines occupy only a scattered 11 hectares of heavy
or gravelly soil, on the limit of the Moulis appellation for the most part. Since the
creation of the "château" in 1819, the same family has run this estate, typical of the
Listrac style of agricultural economy, and carefully preserves old bottles from before
the last war. The wine of Lalande, aged in oak, has the advantage of a proportion
of grapes from old vines, which give it a delicate nose of crushed fruit provided it
is given time to develop. Tannic, of great substance and deep in colour, it should
be left for several years to show its true qualities and develop the correct fullness
of aroma. The wine can be bought every day at the château, which is absolutely
charming in its setting reminiscent of the Landes, quite unusual in wine country.
Practically all the vintages since 1979 (which was an unquestionable success) are
still available.

Lamorère (Château)   ♙♙♙♙♙

There was a family of Moulis growers in the nineteenth century called Lamorelle.
Have they given their name to this *cru* through a slight phonetic change? It is not

impossible. Before the war Lamorère was known as Ruat-Lamorère and already belonged to the Cazeaus. Today René Cazeau is dead, but his wife Antoinette and his children still own 5 hectares of vines in the little locality of Piquey in Moulis. Do not confuse this Piquey with the one on the Bay of Arcachon. The estate of Piquey already featured on the land register at the beginning of the century, producing 30 casks of wine. Although smaller today, the vineyard of Lamorère upholds this ancient tradition.

La Mouline (Château)

Cru bourgeois

Commune: Moulis-en-Médoc. **Proprietor:** GFA Coubris. Manager: Jean-Louis Coubris. Consultant oenologist: Pierre Bariteau, Castelnau. **Size of vineyard:** 15 hectares. **Average age of vines:** 15 years. **Varieties:** 48% cabernet-sauvignon, 4% cabernet-franc, 45% merlot, 3% petit-verdot. **Production:** 65 *tonneaux,* 78,000 bottles CB. **Visits:** by appointment. Jean-Louis Coubris, 72, avenue Pasteur, 33600 Pessac. **Marketing:** 20% through the trade only.

In a region of mills it is not unusual to come across a Château La Mouline, and this one is all the easier to find because there actually is an old mill here. The estate has been managed since 1982 by a Groupement Foncier Agricole of which Jean-Louis Coubris and his son Jean-Christophe are the principal members. But the vineyard has been in the family for a long time. A *cru bourgeois* in 1932, it was gradually reduced from 9 to 3 hectares. The Coubris have now increased it to about 15 hectares. Half the land is on clayey limestone and sandy gravel, unsuitable for anything but vines.

Jean-Louis Coubris has always been in love with growing and oenology. He makes a rather virile wine, slightly austere and marked by the cabernet. The 82s and 83s seem to be developing slowly and should be left to open up. But La Mouline is undergoing a revival and without doubt we can expect improvements. And we can trust the Coubris to devote themselves to the task of producing a little Moulis of good quality.

As for the old mill of La Mouline – one of the most visible monuments in the Moulis countryside – it is quite impossible to miss it. Overlooking the regular rows of vines from the top of its lovely hill, it stands right at the border of the Listrac appellation, which it seems to guard like a sentinel.

La Rose de Graves (Clos)

Commune: Moulis-en-Médoc. **Proprietor:** Monsieur Bernard Porcheron. Consultant oenologist: Monsieur Jacques Boissenot, Lamarque. **Size of vineyard:** 2 hectares. **Average age of vines:** 15 years. **Varieties:** 40% cabernet-sauvignon, 60% merlot. **Production:** 6,000 bottles CB. **Visits:** by appointment only, Monsieur Bernard Porcheron, tel. 56 88 81 36. **Direct sales:** Château La Rose de Graves, Petit-Poujeaux, Moulis-en-Médoc, 33480 Castelnau-de-Médoc. **Marketing:** through the Bordeaux trade.

*label not
communicated*

Between Moulis and Listrac, near the famous Château Clarke, lies Bernard Porcheron's estate, Clos La Rose de Graves, which he inherited only relatively recently, in 1980. The preponderance of merlot gives a supple, round and fruity wine which asks no more than to mature and which deservedly earned its proprietor the gold medal at the Foire de Bordeaux of 1986. The Porcherons work as a family team: bottling is done by the proprietor himself, helped by his father-in-law. Congratulations are due to Bernard and Roger Porcheron, whose expertise is as formidable as their marketing skills.

La Salle de Poujeaux (Château)

→ Poujeaux

Les Hauts Marcieux (Château)

→ Lafon

Lestage (Château)

Cru bourgeois

Commune: Listrac-Médoc. **Proprietor:** SCI Château Lestage (Chanfreau Heirs). Directors: Jacqueline and Jean Chanfreau. Vineyard manager: M. Lesca. Manager: Marc Lalande. Cellar master: Paul Valverde. Consultant oenologist: Jacques Boissenot, Lamarque. **Size of vineyard:** 54 hectares. **Average age of vines:** 26 years. **Varieties:** 30% cabernet-sauvignon, 16% cabernet-franc, 52% merlot, 2% petit-verdot. **Production:** 160,000 bottles CB. **Visits:** Monday to Friday, from 8 a.m. to noon and 2 to 5.30 p.m. Tel. 56 58 02 43. **Direct sales and by mail order:** in France. Château Lestage, Listrac-Médoc, 33480 Castelnau-de-Médoc. **Marketing:** sales through selected merchants in Bordeaux and Libourne.

Although records are lacking and therefore we cannot be sure, it seems that Château Lestage could be the work of the nineteenth-century architect Garros, who constructed a great number of similar buildings in the Gironde. Built in about 1870, it is a representative example of the Second Empire style, rich though with clean-cut lines, a style which has its admirers. But the fame and prestige of Château Lestage are less attributable to its tall windows and sculpted façade than to the quality of its wine. Situated exactly halfway between the fire watchtower on the way into Listrac and Château Clarke as the crow flies, it belonged in the nineteenth century to the Saint-Guirons family, which at that time was sole proprietor of a good quarter of the vineyards in Listrac. Lestage successively passed to Louis Eschenauer, then to Gabriel Seynat, a notable Médocain who held the office of *député* and whose son Jean-Pierre today owns the excellent Château Martinens in Cantenac, of which he is mayor.

Today Château Lestage is the home of the Chanfreau family.

In 1962 it was bought by Marcel Chanfreau, who had acquired the neighbouring Fonréaud six months earlier. Originally from the region of Saint-Gaudens, Marcel Chanfreau had come back from Algeria where he had nearly 800 hectares of vines near Sidi-bel-Abbès. At Lestage he displayed the same colonial enthusiasm by successively replanting nearly 40 hectares, so bringing the vineyard today to a total of 55 hectares in one unbroken stretch on the high ground of Puy-de-Menjon. It is Jean Chanfreau, his grandson, who now reigns over the twofold inheritance of Lestage and Fonréaud. It would be an understatement to say that he gives them, as it were, his undivided attention. And yet the two estates should not be confused. Although Jean Chanfreau divides his efforts equally between the two estates, Lestage is different from Fonréaud in having a wine which is more robust and of greater substance. In short, it is the more Listrac-like of the two and can appear rather harsh to people who like more approachable wine. They should keep the Lestage a while in their cellars. If they ignore it for ten years, they will then discover a marvellous wine.

The soil of Lestage is made up partly of gravel from the Pyrenees and partly of clayey limestone. It is adjacent to the Moulis appellation, into which it makes inroads for it includes a tiny parcel of Lestage vines. Jean Chanfreau selects his *cuvée* rigorously, keeping only the best two-thirds; the rest are marketed under a second name, Château Caroline. In view of the extensive improvements made both on the 141 land and in the working buildings, the wine of Lestage, which is a typical Listrac, should quickly regain the place of honour it held last century, at the head of the *crus* of the commune. But this is no easy wine, much less a fashionable one. Its firm and chewy tannins penalize it in tastings where more aromatic and seductive wines always come out ahead. Happily, not all wines are intended to shine at tastings...

Lestage-Darquier (Château)

Cru bourgeois

Commune: Moulis-en-Médoc. **Proprietors:** François, Jean-Michel and Yves Bernard. Director: François Bernard. Consultant oenologist: Jacques Boissenot, Lamarque. **Size of vineyard:** 6 hectares. **Average age of vines:** 20 years. **Varieties:** 48% cabernet-sauvignon, 50% merlot, 2% petit-verdot. **Production:** 20,000 bottles, approximately. **Direct sales and by mail order:** in France. Monsieur François Bernard, Arcins, 33460 Margaux or Bois-de-Séguet, Grand-Poujeaux, Moulis-en-Médoc, 33480 Castelnau-de-Médoc. Tel. 56 58 96 86. **Marketing:** through the trade.

Planted on the west side of the ridge of Grand-Poujeaux with a good southern exposure, Lestage-Darquier's vineyard is one of the oldest in Moulis. Two parcels are situated on the sometimes sandy, sometimes clayey gravel. A third is to be planted which will add some 3 hectares to the present vineyard. The estate was created in the nineteenth century by Monsieur Darquier and then passed to his great-nephew, Hector Bernard, who was mayor of Moulis. Today it is François, Jean-Michel and Yves Bernard who run the family inheritance lovingly and well. Under the watchful eye of the oenologist Jacques Boissenot, the wine is generally well structured, rather powerful and with that hint of finesse which is typical of a good Moulis. Odd years appear to be particularly successful – 79, 83 and 85 are among the vintages most to be recommended. The last few years have been fairly regular, mostly improving, and this maintains the old reputation of this typically familial *cru bourgeois.*

Lestage-Darquier should to be confused with the single name Lestage, firstly because Lestage-Darquier is a Moulis and Lestage is a Listrac, and secondly because people in the commune still remember Maurice Lestage, the former owner of Château Guitignan. Decorated as a result of the wounds he received fighting as an infantryman in the Great War, he was both grower and patriot. And in memory of the hardships of the trenches, he always gave war veterans a huge discount when they bought his wine!

L'Ermitage (Château)

Commune: Listrac-Médoc. **Proprietor:** Roger Thomas. **Size of vineyard:** 3 hectares. **Average age of vines:** 35 years. **Varieties:** 40% cabernet-sauvignon, 50% merlot, 10% petit-verdot. **Production:** 15 *tonneaux.* **Visits:** daily. **Direct sales and by mail order:** in France and abroad. Monsieur Roger Thomas, Donissan, Listrac-Médoc, 33480 Castelnau-de-Médoc.

*label not
communicated*

Liouner (Château)

Cru bourgeois

Commune: Listrac-Médoc. **Proprietor:** GAEC Bosq et Fils. Consultant oenologist: Pierre Bariteau, Castelnau. **Size of vineyard:** 17 hectares. **Average age of vines:** 15 years. **Varieties:** 50% cabernet-sauvignon, 40% merlot, 10% petit-verdot. **Production:** 70 *tonneaux*. **Visits:** from 9 a.m. to noon and 3 to 5 p.m. Tel. 56 58 04 38. **Direct sales and by mail order:** in France and abroad. Château Liouner, Libardac, Listrac-Médoc, 33480 Castelnau-de-Médoc.

Once there was a small grower in Listrac by the name of Renouil, a name very common in the Médoc. Like so many others, he could have given his name to his *cru* and thus to posterity. But he did not. None the less, his name has survived as a result of a cunning piece of juggling – taking the letters of the word Renouil and rearranging them, to give Liouner! If old father Renouil were to return today, he would see that change has not been confined to linguistics. For, while starting with three hectares in 1956, Pierre Bosq now owns six times as much. This is the result of hard work over a long period, restoring the vineyard and buying parcels of land, piece by piece and row by row. With him his son Pascal continues the same policy, and Liouner has every chance of growing even larger in the future.

This estate is one of the most fragmented of all. Some of the vines are at Libardac, one of the hamlets in the extreme west of the appellation bordering the huge forest. Some are close to Fonréaud on the high plateau. There are some next to Clarke,

At Liouner both names and land are turned upside down.

near Lestage; the rest are here, there and everywhere. This means that there is a wide variety of soils and, accordingly, the wine of Liouner undoubtedly represents the very synthesis of Listrac geology. It is a clayey, chalky, sandy, gravelly wine. Indeed the gravel and cabernet together determine the wine's character. It should be noted that in the middle of this irresistible jigsaw-puzzle of land there is the vineyard of the old Clos Cantegric, a small vineyard (about 4 hectares) which was well known at the beginning of the century but which is now in the hands of the *coopérative*. The Bosqs have made a second label of Cantegric (a great success, moreover), which should not be confused with Laffitte-Cantegric nor with Cantegril, the name of a former mayor of Listrac who was once the owner of Château Clarke.

The wines of Liouner have their partisans and their detractors. Vinified in the old style in cement vats, then aged in wood, it is a deep-coloured wine, powerful, of great substance, almost athletic. Some drinkers dislike this robust quality, but it is typical of Listrac and deserves to be kept for several years in the cellar for the power of the tannins to give place to a round finish. But apart from this characteristic muscular vigour, Liouner is at the top of the league with an elegant bouquet, tremendously long in the mouth, fruity and full. The well-known footballer Patrick Battison is one of Liouner's customers and he claims to detect a particularly delightful hint of violets. This is not the result of mere chance...

Malbec Lartigue (Château) 🛢

→ *Mayne Lalande*

Malmaison (Château)

Malmaison has had an eventful history for many years. The property lies next to Château Anthonic, but the vineyard, straddling the two appellations, has sometimes had a Moulis label and sometimes a Listrac. Today the restrictions imposed by the INAO and the aspirations of the new owner, Baron Edmond de Rothschild (see Château Clarke) have confirmed Malmaison as a Moulis. The name disappeared completetly for some fifteen years, which was a pity, for I remember a delicious Malmaison 73. A new label has reappeared with the arrival of the 88 vintage, proudly announcing that this *cru* has returned to join the wines of the Médoc, and heralding Baron Edmond de Rothschild's arrival in the Moulis appellation. The wine is carefully attended by Jean-Claude Boniface and Jacques Boissenot. This is truly an authentic renaissance. Good news all round.

Maucaillou (Château)

Commune: Moulis-en-Médoc. **Proprietor:** SC Agricole des Domaines du Château Maucaillou. Director: Philippe Dourthe. Vineyard manager: Francis Coulary. Cellar master: Jean-Marc Gobinau. Consultant oenologist: M. Guimberteau. **Size of vineyard:** 60 hectares. **Average age of vines:** 18 years. **Varieties:** 56% cabernet-sauvignon, 35% merlot, 2% cabernet-franc, 7% petit-verdot. **Production:** 330 *tonneaux*, 360,000 bottles CB. **Visits:** Monday to Friday from 9 a.m. to noon and 3 to 5 p.m. Weekends by appointment. Tel. 56 58 04 15. **Direct sales and by mail order:** in France and abroad. Château Maucaillou, Moulis-en-Médoc, 33480 Castelnau-de-Médoc. **Marketing:** 76% through the Bordeaux trade, 24% direct from the château to private customers and firms.

"Up to the age of eighteen, I had hardly ever drunk any wine. And then, one day, my father suggested that I should taste a wine he had opened for his friends. It was a Latour 45. I drank some, and apparently cried 'So that is wine?! Well, I'm with you from now on!" That was how Philippe Dourthe became a *négociant* and grower, like his father before him. If, in the same circumstances, he were to have tasted a Maucaillou 82 or 83, he would probably have reacted in the same way. For through the joint efforts of Monsieur Dourthe and his son, this *cru* has never ceased to improve in quality and is now unquestionably at the same level as a (good) *cru classé*.

Maucaillou takes its name from a little locality on Grand Poujeaux's land register. It means "poor pebble" in the sense intended by the farmers of earlier days: unfit for growing crops. But these poor soils and gravelly land suit vines particularly well, and here the vines are positively spoilt. However, when Roger Dourthe and his brother André bought Maucaillou in 1929, there were only three hectares of vines. The estate essentially comprised large cellars belonging to the *négociant* Petit-Laroche and could house eight thousand casks. Monsieur Petit-Laroche had had them built there in 1871 because of the proximity to the railway station of Moulis-Listrac: the horses had to draw their carts only a few steps to take the wine on the first part of its journey to Bordeaux. Four years later, in 1875, this extraordinary builder had the present château constructed, between the cellars and the railway, as a birthday present for his wife. It is a strange mixture of different styles of architecture, just as wine results from different grapes with elements of the classical, the baroque, the eighteenth century and Napoleon III. It combines touches of the seaside villa with the air of an aristocratic dwelling and a pinch of the Renaissance. Since Roger Dourthe's death in 1984 it is no longer inhabited, but *chambres d'hôte* are shortly to be created to accommodate the ever-increasing number of visitors to the vineyards of Moulis.

So in 1929 the Dourthes became proprietors of an impressive conglomeration of buildings destined more for the *négociant-éleveur* than the vigneron. The family was already local, for at that time Georges, their father, was the owner of Moulin à Vent and was also a merchant, like his own father who in about 1840 had come "up" to Bordeaux from his native Landes. The Dourthe thus have roots in the *département* of the Landes, fact which is not without importance. It could explain Philippe Dourthe's highly colourful personality: an impressive figure with a cigar always between his lips, who works fifteen hours a day and has a new idea every

The case has been made: Maucaillou is a great wine.

week, jovial, impetuous, brusque yet gentle all at the same time. In short, a true Gascon. Under his management the life of Maucaillou has taken a particularly spectacular turn. The vineyard has increased from 15 hectares in 1961 to 60 hectares today. A huge cellar, one of the biggest in the Médoc, can house 2,500 casks, of which half are of new wood. Improvements are constantly being made to the working buildings, which cover a total area of no less than a hectare. Among them is a bottling shed, and many other *crus* from the neighbourhood come to use this facility. A magnificent little museum of wine and vines has been created and is well worth a visit, even a detour, for people wanting to steep themselves in the long history of vine-growing. Philippe Dourthe has shown as much enthusiasm in creating this remarkable museum as in his thesis on oenology, devoted to the complex subject of the osmosis between oak and wine. A enthusiastic sailor, he has crossed the Atlantic several times, generally alone but also once with his father when the latter was 72. A keen sportsman too, he is the only proprietor of a Bordeaux *grand cru* to rent a box in the football stadium at Bordeaux to enable himself, his friends, children or clients to watch the Girondins play. And it was he who created a sort of wine brotherhood, the Maîtres Celliers de Bordeaux, to honour and bring together true wine professionals, cellar masters and cellarmen. The various events take place in the hall called "la salle des Notables", yet another of Philippe Dourthe's creations, inaugurated by local eminent people, with the purpose of promoting the estate's wines. Finally the man is also an artist in his spare time. Included among his works are ten large canvases narrating the outstanding episodes of the history of the wines of Bordeaux since the time of Ausonius. These paintings are hung in the large entrance hall of the museum and therefore seen by thousands of visitors each year. It was here that Philippe Dourthe, elected president of the Moulis *syndicat viticole* in 1990, received the growers and personalities of the Médoc for the tasting and approval of the 1989 vintage.

Maucaillou is the largest viticultural estate in Moulis. This is mainly thanks to the nineteenth-century enthusiasm for building, but also to the impetus given it by the Dourthes and the increase in the area of vines in production. Proof of this is the vat-house installed in 1976, a time when stainless steel was just beginning to make a timid appearance to replace wood and cement. This technical contribution, like that of the large-scale use of new wood, has given a rapid boost to the wine's fame, even in off-years. "In 1984," Philippe Dourthe recalls, "I spent my nights beside my vats. Vinification was difficult and I watched over it closely. I vinified at a low temperature for two days, about 23 degrees, to capture all the aromas I could. Then I let it rise. This has been my method since 1982." The result is that, in comparative tastings, the Maucaillou 84 has every chance of coming out among the leaders. It seems that this technique was responsible for its success in the annual competition of the Médoc *bourgeois* – a friendly contest patronized by Gault et Millau – which it won in 1986, nearly one hundred years after Maucaillou's first gold medal at the Universal Exhibition in Paris in 1889.

With harvests that are often late (it is not uncommon to pick the last of the petit-verdot at the beginning of November), modern installations and rigorous selection (there are two second labels, of which one is a table wine), Maucaillou has made its way slowly but surely to the top. It is now one of the three best in the appellation, along with Poujeaux and Chasse-Spleen, though in certain years their position could well be challenged by *crus* such as Moulin à Vent or Gressier. It is still rather too soon to judge, but the 86 has a rare concentration and power. The 85 is already exceptional in its bouquet, finesse and persistence. The 83 is very stylized and rich, but rather lighter, more gentle and yielding than the others. The 82 and the 81 are classics, full and complex, which can be kept for twenty years and more. And then there is the intensely concentrated 88. There is no point in going on. The case has been made: Château Maucaillou is unquestionably a great wine.

Mauvesin (Château)

Commune: Moulis-en-Médoc. **Proprietor:** André de Baritault. Tenant: Société Viticole de France, Château du Grava, 33550 Haux. Tel. 56 67 23 89. Director: Jean-Luc Dualé. Vineyard manager: Pierre Cariat. Cellar master: Nicolas Leclair. **Size of vineyard:** 60 hectares. **Average age of vines:** 12 years. **Varieties:** 50% cabernet-sauvignon, 5% cabernet-franc, 40% merlot, 5% petit-verdot. **Production:** 370,000 bottles CB. **Visits:** Nicolas Leclair, tel. 56 58 24 28. **Direct sales:** Château Mauvesin, Moulis-en-Médoc, 33480 Castelnau-de-Médoc. **Marketing:** through Bordeaux.

Monsieur and Madame Alain de Baritault and their children.

The ancient and noble house of Mauvesin has its roots in the medieval history of the canton of Castelnau. Going back as far as we can, we find that the "new château" (whence "Castelnau") was built in about the eleventh century, intended to protect the Médoc from Saxon or Norman invasions. The fortresses of Blanquefort and Lesparre were already in existence, but an intermediary stronghold was needed between the two. The château of Castelnau served this purpose, standing by the peninsula's one main road, originally a Roman way, La Lébade. In the year of grace 1108, if we are to believe the Abbé Baurein, a certain Rolland de Castelnau appeared on the scene, a sign that the seigniory was already inhabited. Afterwards the proprietors were the lords Puypaulin, then Pierre de Bordeaux in the thirteenth century and finally the house of Grély, which was allied to the Comtes de Foix. The Abbé Baurein tells us that, "the House of Grély, originally from Gex near Geneva, enjoyed great esteem at the English Court." But after 1453 and the Battle of Castillon, the said English Court no longer held sway over Aquitaine and a new period of history began. That same year, the château of Castelnau was besieged for a fortnight before surrendering to the King of France's soldiers. This created a tremendous stir in the surrounding countryside and it is said that the local people, shouting "Listrac, flee! Castelnau has fallen!", were the first to realize that a page in France's history had just been turned.

In his study of feudal Médoc the Bordeaux genealogist Michel Smaniotto examines in detail the great seigniories from the eleventh to the fifteenth centuries. Here
148 we meet Gombaud de Pommiers, lord of Calon and Mauvesin, and other noble

lords from Lamarque, Lesparre, Arsac and so on. The lord of Castelnau ruled over the parishes of Moulis, Listrac, Bouqueyran and even up to Le Porge and Salaunes. We also know that in 1428 a certain Bertrand de Sarnac was the tithe-owner of the village of Mauvesin, which belonged to the powerful Jean de Foix de Candale et de Béarn, the lord of Buch from the fifteenth century. This Jean de Foix was none other than the lord of Castelnau, the neighbouring barony. The wheel had turned full circle. Mauvesin remained in this family for many years but then was sold in 1647 to Pierre Le Blanc, a member of the Parlement de Bordeaux. It was one of his heirs who in 1853 had the château of today constructed, a beautiful, elegant, unostentatious building in attractive grounds. Unlike the neighbouring village of Bouqueyran (formerly Bécoyran), that of Mauvesin no longer exists, but the Baritault-du-Carpia family who live on the estate today firmly uphold the noble traditions attached to one of the oldest properties in the Médoc. The wine is not lacking in nobility either, and in 1850 Mauvesin was one of the top three Moulis *crus*, along with Poujeaux and Gressier. In 1920 it was the largest producer in the commune, with 175 *tonneaux*. Today it produces twice this amount from 60 hectares in one unbroken stretch and so, with Maucaillou, can be considered as the biggest vineyard in the appellation. Since 1974 the Société Viticole de France, which also runs Château Bernones at Cussac, has managed the Mauvesin vineyard. The vines have been largely replanted over the last fifteen or so years. Modern vinification equipment and a cellar for ageing are some of the more recent investments made to improve the quality of the wine. It is an impressive wine with a good bouquet, typical of Moulis in coming from vines planted in land of clayey limestone or clayey gravel. Because of its deep roots in the region, Château Mauvesin has a place apart in the history of the Médoc. Its wine, which even when very young is characterized by a pleasant smoothness, deserves its own place as well in the cellar of the lover of Moulis wines.

Mayne Lalande (Château)

Commune: Listrac-Médoc. **Proprietor:** Monsieur Bernard Lartigue. **Size of vineyard:** 13 hectares. **Average age of vines:** 25 years. **Varieties:** 50% cabernet-sauvignon, 49% merlot, 1% petit-verdot. **Production:** 70 *tonneaux*, 75,000 bottles CB. **Visits:** daily. Bernard or Dominique Lartigue, tel. 56 58 27 63. **Direct sales and by mail order:** in France and abroad. Le Mayne-de-Lalande, Listrac-Médoc, 33480 Castelnau-de-Médoc. **Marketing:** about 30% through the trade.

Is it true that "artigue" was once the term in Gironde for a peasant who was particularly poor, as some people maintain? Whatever the case, it is certain that the wine of Bernard Lartigue is particularly rich. Mayne Lalande is a new estate whose label first appeared only with the 1982 vintage. A highly original, up-to-date, almost 'fashionable' label, it is in a graphic style as modern as the proprietors. Bernard Lartigue and his wife Dominique settled at Le Mayne in 1973 with just one hectare of vines, whose harvest was vinified at the *coopérative* in Listrac. In less than ten years they created a model estate and a wine which now features among the best of the appellation. To achieve this Bernard Lartigue spared no effort and the amount of work involved is reflected in the spectacular results.

Spectacular too is Mayne Lalande's superb 82, very quickly spotted by capable tasters and in particular by the Bordeaux restaurateur Jean-Pierre Xiradakis. Unknown until then, the wine was surprising in its intensity and quality. Today it is

Bernard Lartigue, a devoted and conscientious vintner.

a remarkable bottle whose very complex nose combines perfumes of crystallized fruit, leather and liquorice. Very long on the palate, full and powerful, you could take it for a *cru classé* at any blind tasting. It is a truly typical Listrac, full-bodied and fruity, but typical too of the efforts made by a whole generation of growers on behalf of their wines.

Bernard Lartigue has also created a *coopérative* for agricultural machinery, to enable its members to have good farming and vinification equipment at their disposal. They are half a dozen in number, all young growers from the canton (Lescoutra, Braquessac, Miquau, Martin, and so on), convinced that there is strength in unity. It is thanks to the efforts of dedicated and conscientious growers like Bernard Lartigue that Listrac can be proud of its young people and its increasing fame.

Clearly we should not imagine that he was satisfied for his 82 to be merely a one-off success. Happily the consumer is more demanding. Following through, Lartigue achieved an honourable, although less concentrated and more austere, 83; a very agreeable 84, which was not easy in that greatly disparaged year; an absolutely sumptuous 85, one of the estate's greatest years which is just beginning to open up; a terribly complex 86, which will take about ten years of ageing to develop. The 88s and 89s are of about the same register, and already appear to be bottles fot laying down.

Mayne Lalande is one of the best wines of Listrac, at once rough and suave, robust and fruity, sturdy and elegant: a great *cru* is being born, and the angels are perched upon its crib...

Moulin à Vent (Château)

Commune: Moulis-en-Médoc. **Proprietor:** M. et Madame Dominique Hessel. Vineyard manager: Guy Baquey. Consultant oenologist: Pauillac Laboratory. **Size of vineyard:** 24.6 hectares. **Average age of vines:** 20 years. **Varieties:** 60% cabernet-sauvignon, 35% merlot, 5% malbec and petit-verdot. **Production:** 120,000 bottles CB. **Visits:** weekdays from 8 a.m. to noon and 2 to 6 p.m. Tel. 56 58 15 79. **Direct sales and by mail order:** in France. Château Moulin à Vent, Moulis-en-Médoc, 33480 Castelnau-de-Médoc. **Marketing:** in France and abroad, sales to private clients. Sole rights to Château Moulin de Saint-Vincent held by Borie-Manoux.

At one time Bouqueyran was one of the liveliest hamlets in the commune of Moulis. It was even an independent parish, if we are to believe in the existence of a church built for the faithful but demolished during the last century (see Fonréaud). Wine has been made at Bouqueyran for as long as can be remembered. Its land, contiguous with Listrac on either side of the Médoc road, is known for being the highest in Moulis. So the name of Moulin à Vent comes as no surprise, though working mills have now become very rare.

In about 1850 a certain Monsieur Brun created this estate by uniting several parcels of land. Forty years later his son enlarged it further both in Moulis and in Listrac. Georges Dourthe, the proprietor at the beginning of the century, also increased the estate's reputation. It should be added that, at the time, Moulin à Vent was producing a semi-sweet white wine, as did many other properties in Listrac or Saint-Laurent. After the Dourthe family, the successive owners were Monsieur Gilbon, Monsieur Kaskoreff and Monsieur Darricarrère. The latter sold the estate in March 1977 to Dominique Hessel, who right from the start displayed a keen passion for this *cru,* the effects of which soon made themselves felt.

Château
Moulin à Vent
MOULIS- MEDOC

Moulin à Vent could not have fallen into better hands. A former pupil of Montpellier's Agricultural College, a qualified oenologist, with a wealth of experience in the vineyards of Gironde, Dominique Hessel came to Moulis with the extra qualification of coming from a growing family which has owned vines in Lalande-de-Pomerol since the fifteenth century. He settled in his new region and proved himself a model grower, for six years later in 1983 he was elected president of the Groupement d'Intérêt Economique des Vins du Médoc, and as such took charge of representing and promoting the peninsula's 1,600 growers. At the same time, 151

Dominique Hessel likes to smell the results of his efforts.

the president took on another vineyard, Château La Tour-Blanche in the north of the Médoc, at Saint-Christoly, so putting down roots in two places in this land for which he has become one of the best ambassadors. For the record it should be noted that at Montpellier Dominique Hessel was a pupil of Jean Branas, a teacher of agronomy of worldwide repute and a specialist in the physiology of vines. He too comes from Moulis (see Château Branas), and his family once owned a parcel of vines now included within the vineyard of Moulin à Vent!

However versatile Dominique Hessel proved, times were difficult at the beginning, especially in the first year. When he harvested the 77 it gave the slender yield of eight hectolitres per hectare, five times less than the appellation's base yield. Fortunately things went much better from then on and today Moulin à Vent is the very model of a perfect blend of indispensable tradition and essential modernization. The cellars and vat-house have been progressively improved, with the introduction of stainless steel and new wood to age the wine for two years. The château itself, an attractive eighteenth-century country house which was uninhabited for some time, has been restored. The vines are not "forced" and the use of fertilizers is not automatic. "I do it by rule of thumb," says the proprietor, who is vineyard manager, cellar master and also in charge of manuring.

The estate has four distinct parcels totalling 25 hectares. The highest, at an altitude of nearly 40 metres, is made up of gravel from the Pyrenees, and the others are of clayey limestone. This mixture is excellent, for the wine of Moulin à Vent, elegant, rich and velvety, is one of the appellation's great successes. Its powerful bouquet with aromas of blackcurrant, its consistency, its capacity for ageing – in a word, its classicism – make it not only a great Moulis but a great Médoc. The 88 and 89 vintages are spectacular successes, compactly constructed, rich and powerful, reminiscent of the succulent 85. This wine is outstanding for its perfect balance between acidity, alcohol, tannin and the concentration of fruit. Moulin à Vent is one of the best buys which the lover of great Médoc wines should, and must, not miss.

Moulin de Laborde (Château)

Cru bourgeois

Commune: Listrac-Médoc. **Proprietor:** S.E.A. du Château Listrac. Consultant oenologist: Jacques Boissenot, Lamarque. **Size of vineyard:** 12 hectares. **Average age of vines:** 26 years. **Varieties:** 60% cabernet-sauvignon, 30% merlot, 10% petit-verdot. **Production:** 65,000 bottles CB. **Visits:** Monday to Friday from 8 a.m. to 8 p.m. For groups of more than twenty people and at weekends, by appointment. M. Hostens, tel. 56 58 03 83. **Direct sales and by mail order:** in France. Château Moulin de Laborde, Listrac-Médoc, 33480 Castelnau-de-Médoc. **Marketing:** 50% for export, 30% through small outlets in France and 20% to private clients.

Michel Hostens is a very engaging person. When he was young, he wanted to become a professional musician and secretly nurtured the hope of going to Paris to play the trombone. Ill-health prevented him and he was obliged to abandon music, turning instead to vines. He quickly became a specialist in grafting and for ten years grafted whole vineyards throughout the canton. At the same time he began to cultivate two hectares of vines given to him by his father-in-law. But two hectares is not much, so Michel Hosten bought one parcel, then another and another, with the result that today Moulin de Laborde consists of 12 hectares. Three-quarters is on pebbly soil round the working buildings, which can be identified from the road by an old mill (soon to be restored) and a huge new wine shed.

He is not the sort of man to put his feet up and, not being satisfied with simply making wine, he also tried to sell it. He succeeded by going to all the coastal resorts in the Médoc during the high season, quickly establishing a faithful clientele (important for launching a private marketing programme) which now knows no frontiers. Still keen to invest in the wine business, Michel Hostens bought a further four hectares in 1977 (see Fourcas-Loubaney) and then acquired a mechanical harvester. "Since I have had the machine, I have improved on quality," he reckons. "For my harvesting depends on the ripeness of the grapes, parcel by parcel, and on the weather." And believe it or not, in order to age his 86 correctly, he bought one hundred new casks in one go, which amply demonstrates his unwillingness to skimp. So, having firmly established a going concern, and installed equipment guaranteeing first-rate vinification, he sold Moulin de Laborde to the Novalliance Group in 1989. The sale also included Fourcas Loubaney, Michel Hosten's other *cru*, though his son Franck remained at the estate as cultivation supervisor, together with Jean-Claude Maubert: two very capable men to maintain continuity.

The wine of Moulin de Laborde comes from one of Listrac's best areas, the Pyrenean gravel on the plateau of Le Fourcas. Even in off-years the old cabernet-sauvignon vines give the wine a delicacy and power which combine elegantly. Recent vintages have been very succesful. They are round, full wines which can confidently be laid down for ten years. This still little-known *cru* deserves to be discovered and watched closely. If the 89 vintage was quite successful at Moulin de Laborde, 1990 has unfortunately started badly. Part of the large *chai* was ravaged in one night 153 by a fire whose flames were visible all the way from the road to Soulac. About twenty thousand bottles were lost, not to mention the heavy damage suffered by the building.

Moulin de Saint-Vincent (Château)

→ *Moulin à Vent*

Moulin du Bourg (Château)

Commune: Listrac-Médoc. **Proprietor:** Monsieur Michel Lescoutra, Listrac-Médoc, 33480 Castelnau-de-Médoc. Tel. 56 58 03 44. Management by GAEC Lescoutra-Miquau. **Size of vineyard:** 12 hectares. **Average age of vines:** 18 years. **Varieties:** 25% cabernet-sauvignon, 60% merlot, 15% petit-verdot. **Production:** 70,000 bottles CB. **Marketing:** vinified at the *cave de vinification*, Listrac, tel. 56 58 03 19.

The Lescoutras have been growers in Listrac for many years. They and the Boscs, Meyres, Hosteins, Raymonds and others are vine-growing dynasties which have retained over the centuries the determination to continue the work of their predecessors. It is not by chance that a Lescoutra is the mayor of the commune today, after succeeding another notable in the local vine-growing world, Henri Bibian. The property of Moulin du Bourg was created by Pierre Bertaud in about 1850, and Michel Lescoutra is the seventh person to own this vineyard whose acreage has doubled in fifteen years. With 12 hectares, of which two are planted with petit-verdot, it is scattered about the village, but the GAEC Miquau-Lescoutra, which we have already met at the Clos du Fourcas, runs the vineyard with devotion and pride. Vinification is carried out at the *cave coopérative*. Recently reelected at the last ballot along with his team, Michel Lescoutra is indeed an ardent defender of viticulture.

Moulis (Château)

Cru bourgeois

Commune: Moulis-en-Médoc. **Proprietor:** Jacques Darricarrère. Estate manager and cellar master: Philippe Darricarrère. Vineyard manager: Miloud Khalaïne. Consultant oenologist: Pierre Bariteau, Castelnau-de-Médoc. **Size of vineyard:** 12 hectares. **Average age of vines:** 30 years. **Varieties:** 60% cabernet-sauvignon, 40% merlot. **Production:** 46 *tonneaux*, 55,000 bottles CB. **Visits:** by appointment preferably. Monsieur Philippe Darricarrère, or Madame Khalaïne, tel. 57 42 25 95 or 57 68 40 01. **Direct sales or by mail order:** in France and abroad. Château Moulis, Moulis-en-Médoc, 33480 Castelnau-de-Médoc. **Marketing:** through the Bordeaux trade.

The vineyard of Château Moulis lies next to the cellar and the house.

Just as there is a Château Margaux in Margaux and a Château Saint-Estèphe in Saint-Estèphe, naturally enough there is a Château Moulis in Moulis. It has been in existence since the nineteenth century, when it was built in the rather classical style typical of such substantial houses in the Gironde. It was already linked to a vineyard, and in 1860 Monsieur Anglas produced thirty *tonneaux* of wine here. In 1920 the estate, extending over 100 hectares of which 12 were under vine, belonged to Maurice Lasserre. Since 1969 Jacques Darricarrère and his son Philippe have looked after the vineyard, still of twelve hectares, on the ridges of Bouqueyran and Larozey. At first they leased the land from the Lasserre heirs, then in 1980 they bought the vineyard after selling the neighbouring property, Moulin à Vent, three years earlier to Dominique Hessel. But once we start to count the estates which belong to or are run by the Darricarrères we quickly become aware that the list is extensive: Château Mille-Secousses ("a thousand shakes") and Château Rider-Chenu-Laffitte in Bourg-sur-Gironde, Château La Barde at Tauriac and Château Mendoce in Villeneuve, together with Château Moulis, make up a very large slice of the wine world in Gironde. This is not to mention the estate on the Ile de Margaux in the Gironde estuary, which was sold in 1969. With all these different labels, whatever the appellation, the Darricarrères are excellent wine makers and they have made a great success of their work with wine in the Bordeaux area.

Despite his name, typical of the Landes, Jacques Darricarrère originally comes from Mâcon, the descendant of a teacher who is said to have taught Lamartine. When his father lived in Algeria, he created a vineyard out of nothing, though he had to abandon it when the country gained its independence. So this colonial family came to the Médoc and the Côte-de-Bourg, bringing with them an unflagging enthusiasm for the land. The wine of Château Moulis is a good classic example of its appellation, in its soil, grape varieties and quality. It does not have the power or the complexity of the *crus* from the gravelly land of Grand-Poujeaux but it quickly develops a suppleness and a great delicacy of bouquet. Philippe Darricarrère is right when he speaks of "persistence in the mouth and tannins which are generally not too aggressive". All this perfectly sums up the qualities of this little *cru*, handled by the Bordeaux trade but also sold to faithful private clients (by mail order).

Peyredon Lagravette (Château)

Cru bourgeois

Commune: Listrac-Médoc. **Proprietor:** Paul Hostein. Consultant oenologist: CEIO, Pauillac. **Size of vineyard:** 7 hectares. **Average age of vines:** 25 years. **Varieties:** 65% cabernet-sauvignon, 30% merlot, 5% malbec. **Production:** 36,000 bottles CB. **Visits:** Saturdays from 9 a.m. to 8 p.m. Other days by appointment. **Direct sales and by mail order:** in France. Château Peyredon Lagravette, Médrac, Listrac-Médoc, 33480 Castelnau-de-Médoc. **Marketing:** wholesale exporters.

At once manager, vineyard manager, cellar master and oenologist on his little estate, Paul Hostein is a typical example of a Médoc grower not so much born as found underneath a vine. When he was a child he used to crush the grapes underfoot with his friends from the village, and as a result of his father's sudden illness in 1950, he was obliged to make his first wine at the age of 19. Since then he has lived for, by and with wine. He carefully tends his forty-year-old vines, does not force the yields or filter excessively, and respects Tradition (with a capital T) with filial, almost religious respect.

You have only to see his cellar, well-ordered, neat and tidy with its old oval casks, *barriques* and old bottles lining the walls, to understand that Paul Hostein loves wine more than money. And how refreshing in this age of technology to come across genuinely hand-crafted wines ! As its two names indicate, Peyredon Lagravette arises from the marriage of two properties. And marriage is the right word, for one belonged to Paul Hostein's father's family and the other to his mother's. As for the derivation of the name, it is simply geological, for "peyredon" means a mound of stones and "gravette" a little pebble. So we need look no further to find the roots of the wine, deep in the excellent Médrac soil of gravel deposited by the Garonne. This is one of the finest terrains in Listrac, though one of the most deceptive too, on several counts: firstly because the soil of Château Peyredon Lagravette is not typical of its appellation, secondly because two hectares are hemmed by the vines of Chasse-Spleen on the ridge of Grand-Poujeaux, and finally because the hamlet of Médrac straddles Moulis and Listrac. This geographical confusion is a real brain-teaser for those lovers of legal quibbles who are ever ready to claim the existence of boundaries which according to traditional custom and practice are purely imaginary. But does it really matter after all?

The Hosteins have always been growers in Listrac and Paul Hostein has inherited an estate which has been in existence since the sixteenth century. In 1546 it belonged to the Chevalier de La Salle, a lord of Poujeaux. And if the "château" was only built in 1868, the oak trees in the forest of Tronçais which still provide the wood for the *barriques* also date from this time. In fact, everything here bears witness to a deep appreciation of tradition.

Quality is all important. For this wine, with its double character representative both of Listrac and Moulis, has the immense virtue of being as good when it is young as when it has aged. The 82 is perfect but then so is the 45. All the vintages since 78 have been praised to the skies. The wine is fruity, round, distinguished, well-structured, velvety and deep in colour, with hints of vanilla and raspberry. Paul Hostein has one of the most impressive collections of press cuttings in the commune and he takes great delight in looking through them on long winter evenings. But this great smallholder has not has his head turned. His warm welcome, his simplicity and affability resemble his wine. So hurry and drop in to see him at Médrac before foreign merchants buy up all his wines. He still has a few bottles (from the 81 vintage on) for the visitor who is prepared to take time to make worthwhile discoveries. The way he speaks of his wine is the best initiation to a tasting. And if you have been very good, he will perhaps show you the venerable collection of stuffed birds created by his grandfather, when heron, snipe and goldfinches also used to come to harvest here. This is his other treasure, and he would not sell this one for all the money in the world.

Peyrelebade (Château)

Commune: Listrac-Médoc. **Proprietor:** Compagnie Vinicole des Barons Edmond et Benjamin de Rothschild. General manager: Jean-Claude Boniface. Estate manager and vineyard manager: D. Roba. Cellar master: Philippe Bonnin. Consultant oenologist: Jacques Boissenot, Lamarque. **Size of vineyard:** 60 hectares. **Average age of vines:** 10 years. **Varieties:** 30% cabernet-sauvignon, 13% cabernet-franc, 57% merlot. **Production:** 100,000 bottles CB. **Direct sales and by mail order:** in France and abroad. Château Peyrelebade, Listrac-Médoc, 33480 Castelnau-de-Médoc.

label not communicated

Peyrelebade is an estate which stands apart from the viticultural geography of Listrac for several reasons, for the past and the present, art and geology all come together here in a singular fashion. Bearing the imprint of two different men – Odilon Redon in the nineteenth century and Edmond de Rothschild in the twentieth – this château (which is such only in name) has an endearing personality born of converging factors. It would be best to consider them separately.

In the nineteenth century Peyrelebade was a classic agricultural estate belonging to the Redon family from Bordeaux. The artist Odilon Redon describes it in his diary, *A soi-même:* "My father owned an old estate surrounded by vines and uncultivated land, with huge trees, broom everywhere and heather coming right up to the château. When I was a child, all we could see from the door was a landscape shrouded in brambles and ferns with the remains of broad avenues planted with elms." The artist spent much of his time at Peyrelebade, where the light of the countryside and the movement of the clouds deeply influenced him: "How fascinated I am by the sky!" He was greatly distressed by the sale of the estate in 1887, when, although it changed hands, it still remained a vine-growing estate. In 1920 the Peyrun-Berron family harvested fifty *tonneaux* of red wine, a quarter of the quantity produced by their mighty neighbour, Château Clarke.

Geologically, the soil of Peyrelebade is made up of Tertiary limestone, together with clay, sand or silex depending on the area. These varying strata are simply the remains of a mound that has been hollowed out: a natural depression believed to be a geological accident by the greatest experts. The original existence of this mound, now eroded, was also accidental. It is generally accepted that the vein of limestone here is the same as that found on the other side of the estuary on the right bank. And we know that there was once a stone quarry at Peyrelebade, as there was also in Bourg-sur-Gironde.

Phonetically Peyrelebade is an attractive name, but completely unpronounceable for English-speakers, a fact which gives rise to marketing problems (we shall come back to this). Local linguistic tradition pronounces it "Pay-rer-ler-bad" which is difficult for a citizen of Albuquerque, however fond of wine he may be. It seems that the etymology of the word is "raised stone", which accords in with local dialect 157 and means that there might have been some sort of menhir here. And as we know that there was once a dolmen a few hundred yards away on the plateau of Les Marcieux, the explanation is plausible. But the existence of a stone quarry throws yet another possible light on the derivation of the name.

Viticulturally, Peyrelebade is again what it once was, after a long period during which its prestige declined. Baron Edmond de Rothschild, then the proprietor of Clarke for five years, bought the estate's 90 hectares in 1979 and immediately gave it a new lease on life. The most obvious effect was the progressive planting of 60 hectares of vines, after the reorganization of each parcel and the installation of an effective drainage system. Given its area, the creation of this vineyard was one of the largest undertakings of its type in any appellation in the Gironde.

Nor was there any intention of keeping all this in the dark, as demonstrated by the sumptuous reception given here by Nadine and Edmond de Rothschild in the spring of 1985 in honour of the exhibition organized by the May Music Festival in Bordeaux entitled "Homage to Odilon Redon". Jacques Chaban-Delmas, surrounded by a thousand leading lights in the world of art, wine and politics, unveiled a commemorative plaque on the wall of the house where the painter lived, then everyone moved off to a banquet in the cellars of Château Clarke. It should also be mentioned that it was the Edmond-de-Rothschild Foundation which financed the transport of Redon's pictures, lent by American art collectors, from New York to Bordeaux where they were put on exhibition. Finally another sign of Peyrelebade's international renown came when Japanese scientists arrived in 1986 to study the estate's soil and subsoil, commonly known as Peyrelebade's "limestone buttonhole". Commercially, the label of "Domaine de Peyrelebade" represents neither a second label, nor a pale imitation of Clarke, but a wine in its own right with a distinct personality. In the 1985 vintage it adorned a production limited to 36,000 magnums, reserved for private customers. But in other years, and notably in the last few vintages, this wine has assumed an independant existence, under the vigilant eye of Jean-Claude Boniface. At Peyrelebade he has introduced the same management by individual parcels, the same criteria for selection and the same vinification methods as at Clarke.

In the future, production should not exceed ten thousand boxes of a wine considered much more supple than that of Clarke and more marked by the merlot. While waiting to see what the still young vines will give tomorrow, we should acknowledge the spectacular renaissance of Peyrelebade, where Odilon Redon made another entry in his diary, in the form of a meditation: "It seems that those who belong to the land are under the spell of an occult power, working obscurely but beneficially as long as is necessary for its treasures – a sort of retributive law imposed without their knowledge, for man's delight."

Pierre Bibian (Château)

Commune: Listrac-Médoc. **Proprietor:** Jean Tigana. Vineyard manager: Jean-Pierre Mallet. Cellar master: Jean-Michel Monnet. Consultant oenologist: Jacques Boissenot, Lamarque. **Size of vineyard:** 17 hectares. **Average age of vines:** 30 years. **Varieties:** 35% cabernet-sauvignon, 50% merlot, 15% petit-verdot. **Production:** the estate is just starting production. **Visits:** Tel. 56 58 05 47 by appointment only. **Direct sales and by mail order:** Château Pierre Bibian, Monsieur Jean Tigana, Listrac, 33480 Castelnau-de-Médoc.

*label not
communicated*

The centre-forward Jean Tigana in the centre of his vines.

The Bibians wrere one of the best-known families in Listrac, firstly because they had owned vines in the commune from the beginning of the nineteenth century, and secondly because two of them became mayors of the village. This *cru* bears the name of the man who created it in 1857, linking the vineyard he had inherited from his father with the one that he had from his father-in-law, Monsieur Lambert. It was then known by the name of Cru Fourcas-et-Baudan, the gravelly soil of Baudan being famous for the fine wines it produced. Succeeding generations here have been anxious to carry on the example of their ancestor. Classed as a *bourgeois supérieur* in 1932, this *cru* figured for a long time among the best labels in the commune. The wine was well-structured, typical of Listrac but with a bouquet and delicacy deriving from very old and carefully tended vines, which were largely responsible for its fame. The death of Henri Bibian, shortly after the municipal elections in 1983 in which the people of Listrac had voted him back into office, marked a turning point in the history of the property since there was no direct descendant to inherit it. So began a difficult period, making a sale inevitable. But a purchaser still had to be found.

One appeared in quite an unexpected way in the person of the football player Jean Tigana. It is no secret that he is one of the best centre-forwards in the world, an indefatigable player of rare poise, skill and rapidity, who has played in more than fifty international matches. Jean Tigana, nicknamed Jeannot, that unshakeable pillar of the Bordeaux team, the Girondins, with whom he has enjoyed such success, had been wanting to buy a wine-producing estate in the Gironde for some time. He had visited several but he was taken straight away with Pierre Bibian. He was also impressed by the increasing prestige of the Listrac appellation, another reason for trying his hand in this field, as new as it was attractive. Jean Tigana became a viticulturalist at the beginning of 1987, though he did not abandon football, for that same year, in blue and white stripes, he was once again France's champion of the first division. With great enthusiasm, the new proprietor began to learn about 159 and love wine – though not to drink it, for he has to keep to a very strict diet to keep in shape. Within a few months he had become a fully-fledged member of the great family of Listrac wine, into which he was welcomed with spontaneous warmth and admiration. The fact that he was an unrivalled star on the sports field has not affected his modest and unassuming desire to become part an appellation for which he has at the same time become a living advertisement.

But what he wanted most of all was to do as well in a field unknown to him as on the field of play. He at once initiated extensive improvements, first of all in the vineyard, split into several parcels: one by the side of Clarke and Lestage, the others near Fourcas Hosten on the famous gravelly soil of Baudan. After completely draining the heavy clayey land, he has put in hand a three-year programme for replanting 6 hectares with new vines, so bringing the total vineyard area up to 20 hectares. Then he restored and renovated the working buildings, which stand in the village in the rue d'Eglise. A pleasant reception and tasting room has been opened, the cellars and vat-house have a more attractive appearance and, overall, Pierre Bibian has taken on a new lease of life. Yet although the name of the *cru* has benefited from the prestige of the new owner, it will be used only for the more ordinary wine produced by the château in future. For it is an old name of the Bibian family, Château Laffitte-Cantegric (see above), which is to grace the label of the best wines of what is locally now called Château Tigana. Hardly had this become known than the *négociants* in Bordeaux, who up to that time had been rather reserved about Listrac wines, displayed a sudden interest in the champion's wine, whose very name on the label would ensure success. But we can trust Jean Tigana not to be swayed by flattery. His experience of competition and his wish to succeed are the best guarantee for the *cru* he has taken on. Moreover, the team spirit he has always shown on the field will quite naturally come into play once more alongside the growers of the village, to the appellation's general renown. Pierre Bibian is dead but its wine has been born again in new guise, with promising guarantees for its future.

Following another season crowned with success in the French league championship in the strip of the Olympique de Marseille, Jean Tigana is now starting to prepare for his retirement from football, and his entry into the world of active viticulture, where he is awaited with pleasure.

Pomeys (Château)

Cru bourgeois

Commune: Moulis-en-Médoc. **Proprietor:** Xavier Barennes. Vineyard manager: Véronique Barennes. Consultant oenologist: Bernard Couasnon, Laboratoire oenologique de Pauillac. **Size of vineyard:** 8 hectares. **Average age of vines:** 22 years. **Varieties:** 70% cabernet-sauvignon, 30% merlot. **Production:** 35,000 bottles CB. **Visits:** everyday from 9 a.m. to 7 p.m. Sundays by appointment only. M. Barennes, tel. 56 58 24 85. **Direct sales and by mail order:** in France and abroad. Château Pomeys, Moulis-en-Médoc, 33480 Castelnau-de-Médoc. **Marketing:** through the trade in France and abroad.

Xavier Barenne uncontestably makes good wine, but he also is remarkably well-versed in history, for he can recite the names of all the proprietors of his estate since 1452, with the maiden names of their spouses, the nicknames of their beaux and the professions of their sons-in-law. Such detailed knowledge comes from the

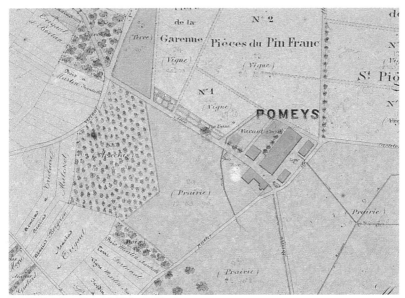

An old land register of Château Pomeys.

Barennes' close attachment to their estate: as the seventh generation of the same family in Moulis their roots go deep, naturally forging strong bonds with the region of their birth.

First of all, there was the noble house of Pomeys belonged to the Chevalier de l'Isle in the Middle Ages. Then, in the seventeenth century, came the powerful lord Gaspard de Courtenay, followed in 1658 by Magdelaine de Durfort, his widow. Thereafter there followed a string of noble lords at Pomeys, including Marshal de Duras and Chevalier Guillaume de Mallet. In the nineteenth century the estate came into the hands of the Barennes family through the female line. Monsieur Dubos, the Bordeaux *négociant*, increased the property to 300 hectares and planted six thousand vines, enlarged the working buildings and had a vat-house built in 1878. From that time on Pomeys became one of Moulis's leading *crus* and was exported abroad. From 1880 it was exported to Berlin and, as proof of its ability to travel, a hundred years later it went round the world aboard a sailing-ship with Eric Tabarly at the helm.

One of Emile Peynaud's pupils at the Bordeaux Oenological Institute, who then trained at Château Margaux, Xavier Barennes today makes a wine which is worthy of its long-established reputation. It is one of the most refined of Moulis wines, and with its delicacy, fine aromas of raspberry and its elegant supple roundness it is reminiscent of the *crus* of the Haut-Médoc appellation nearest to Margaux. In this respect it is typical of the traditional delicacy of Moulis wines, made from a high proportion of cabernet planted on gravelly soil. Pomeys, which was a *cru bourgeois supérieur* in 1932, is sold direct at the château. You cannot miss it, for it is the first estate on your left as you leave Castelnau. It has the distinguishing feature of being the furthest to the south and west of all Moulis's wines. And Pomeys has one more advantage: you can drink it relatively young, for it does not need ten years to open up – although it can easily be kept twenty years if you happen to forget you have some in your cellar. But it would be a pity not to take advantage of the wine while it still displays the full freshness of its fruity flavours and the pleasing firmness of its tannins.

Poujeaux (Château)

Commune: Moulis-en-Médoc. **Proprietor:** Theil family trust. Directors: Philippe, Jean-Pierre and François Theil. Vineyard manager: Franck Antoldi. Cellar master: Daniel Bercion. Consultant oenologist: Jacques Boissenot, Lamarque. **Size of vineyard:** 50 hectares. **Average age of vines:** 30 years. **Varieties:** 45% cabernet-sauvignon, 10% cabernet-franc, 35% merlot, 10% petit-verdot. **Production:** 250,000 bottles CB. **Visits:** from 9 a.m. to noon and 2 to 6 p.m. François Theil, tel. 56 58 02 96. **Direct sales and by mail order:** in France. Château Poujeaux, Moulis-en-Médoc, 33480 Castelnau-de-Médoc. **Marketing:** through distributors with sole rights.

Château Poujeaux: the cellar for the new wine.

The noble and powerful lord Gaston de L'Isle, Baron de La Brède et de Beautiran and lord of many lands in the Médoc, was the first known proprietor of the noble house of La Salle-de-Poujeaux. That was in 1544. At that time Poujeaux was written Poujaulx, and we have every reason to believe that there was already a small vineyard on this hillock of poor, dry gravelly soil. Sixty years later, at the dawn of the seventeenth century, La Salle-de-Poujeaux belonged to a certain Denis de Mullet, who was also proprietor of the noble house of Saint-Mambert, in other words Château Latour at Pauillac. It then passed into the hands of the Marquis de Brassier, the lords of Beychevelle, then to one of their sisters, Madame de Montmorin Saint-Herem, and then to Monsieur André Castaing, who bought it on July 18, 1806. After this it took the name of Château Poujeaux and quickly became the commune's largest producer. Around 1850 it was not uncommon for it to harvest a quarter of the whole of the vintage declared in Moulis. From 1880 onwards the estate was divided into three – Poujeaux-Castaing, Poujeaux-Marly and Poujeaux-Thibault. There was even a Poujeaux-Jacmart at the beginning of the century, not to mention the Clos Poujeaux belonging to Henri Ducasse. Today Château Poujeaux has been brought under one wing and is now as it used to be, although it

The Theil brothers make an eminently successful team.

still has a three-sided aspect in the form of the three brothers, Philippe, François and Jean-Pierre Theil, the present owners and directors of a vineyard which stretches over some 50 hectares and employs twenty-five people.

Like many other Libourne growers, the Theils come from Corrèze, where they were wine-merchants. Grandfather François Theil came and settled in the Bordeaux area when he bought Château Le Pape in Léognan in 1903. He sold it in 1920, though still keeping up his activities as a merchant, came to Moulis and bought a third of Château Poujeaux, which was divided up at that time. Not until 1967 did his son, Jean Theil, acquire the last third, Poujeaux-Thibault and reunite the estate again. Until his death in 1981 Jean Theil was one of the most remarkable people in the appellation and possibly in the whole of the wine world of the Médoc. A remarkable wine maker, he was also an accomplished oenologist without knowing it and even in off-years managed to produce wines of note. One of wine's great protagonists, he was a pillar of the Commanderie du Bontemps de Médoc et des Graves, furthering its aims with energy and dedication. But in particular he made Poujeaux one of the best of all the Moulis wines, and one of the most outstanding of all the *crus bourgeois* in the Médoc – those which would undoubtedly be classified if ever the 1855 list were to be revised. Poujeaux would certainly deserve to be included. Jean Theil handed on his talent and convictions to his three sons, but the Médoc will never forget that behind his small stature there was a great man.

It is rather difficult to define the wine of Grand-Poujeaux, other than by calling it simply a perfect synthesis. The *cru* is situated at the centre of the ridge of Grand-Poujeaux, which geographically speaking is more or less at the very centre of the Haut-Médoc. It has the same soil as the Grands Crus classés, and its climate is also similar, if we overlook the harsh frosts which occur beside the estuary. The choice of grape varieties too is typical of the Médoc: cabernet-sauvignon and merlot dominate but the 5 hectares of petit-verdot and cabernet-franc are a useful boost in certain years. The whole of the harvest is not automatically used for the final wine, but at least three-quarters goes into the final *cuvée*. The vines are planted in the traditional manner, ten thousand plants per hectare, in accordance with the precept of "one metre by one metre" that reigned before the arrival of the mechanical harvester. Pruning keeps the vines low so that the grapes can benefit from the sun's heat reflected on to them by the pebbles in the soil. The wine is fined with egg-whites, but not filtered. A third of the casks are renewed yearly, temperatures are controlled mechanically for vinification and the wine can be left to age for ten, twenty or fifty years, according to choice. A fine instance of this is the astonishing Poujeaux 70 whose youth and vigour demonstrate that it is winning the long challenge that it has thrown down to time. This wine represents a remarkable example of successful ageing over two decades.

It is this conjunction of various factors – geological, natural, human, technical and agricultural – which makes Poujeaux a synthesis of everything which is done traditionally, together with only the best of new techniques, in the Grands Crus of the Médoc. In certain years, such as 1977, Poujeaux is unique and can be as elegant and delicate as a Margaux and as powerful and complex as a Saint-Julien. More often than not it has grace and delicacy, but it can sometimes surprise with its robust structure, much resembling a Pauillac. If we except the really poor years, it will always have a future in front of it, even if the bottle is already thirty years old. That is one of its secrets, or rather its mysteries. It is doubtless the result of an astonishing balance which in the glass gives it an exceptional harmony of aromas. You should drink this wine at least once in your life, but several times would be even better.

Renouil Franquet (Château) ⚗ → *Bel Air Lagrave*

Reverdi (Château)

Commune: Listrac-Médoc. **Proprietor:** Christian Thomas. Consultant oenologist: Jacques Boissenot, Lamarque. **Size of vineyard:** 11.9 hectares. **Average age of vines:** 25 years. **Varieties:** 47% cabernet-sauvignon, 3.5% cabernet-franc, 46% merlot, 3.5% petit-verdot. **Production:** 55 *tonneaux*, 66,000 bottles CB. **Visits:** everyday except Sunday from 9 a.m. to 6 p.m. **Direct sales and by mail order:** in France and abroad. Château Reverdi, Listrac-Médoc, 33480 Castelnau-de-Médoc. Tel. 56 58 02 25. **Marketing:** approximately 90% in Europe.

The Thomas family have long been growers in Donissan, where the land is supposed to have been the first in Listrac to be planted with vines. Grandfather Jules was already living there at the time and had one of the village's main cooperages. After the First World War, he created a little vineyard which his two sons enlarged and divided up, Roger taking Château l'Ermitage and Georges Château Reverdi. Curiously enough, these two names were already in existence – but in the Haut-Médoc. Since the creation of the communal appellations, they have belonged exclusively to Listrac. Today Christian Thomas, Georges's son, directs Château Reverdi, which takes its name from an old Lamarque estate. The vineyard covers some dozen hectares in different parcels with two types of terrain. At Fourcas and Laborde, the vines are on gravel from the Pyrenees. At Les Marcieux, they are on clay and stones, bordering the vineyards of Gobinaud and Lafon. There are several rows of cabernet-franc planted in 1934: their yield is low and of good quality, and the grapes have such a concentrated juice that Christian Thomas looks after these *vieilles vignes* with special care.

Since 1981, Reverdi's wine owes much to the efforts made by the proprietor to improve its quality. It is a tannic but very fruity wine, with hints of vanilla, which is aged for eighteen months before bottling, sometimes in wood and sometimes

Christian Thomas among newly planted vines.

in the vat. Despite being robust, it is not aggressive and new wood gives it an added perfume and charm. It is a true Listrac which marries power with delicacy. The twofold secret of this success is Christian Thomas's perfectionist approach and the advice of the oeonologist Jacques Boissenot. Not just a grower and wine maker, Christian Thomas also distributes his own wine. Ninety per cent is taken by private clients all over Europe. A second label, Château La Gravette, has recently been created for the export market, though this does not rule out direct sales at the château, which gladly opens its doors to visitors. Château Reverdi is making constant progress. It is not yet a very well-known name but it is clear that it soon will be. The 88s and the 89s are absolutely superb and are of outstanding concentration and complexity. Christian Thomas is in the process of increasing the size of his domaine and in a few years will be able to count on a greater volume of production. Thus will he also be able to satisfy the demands of even more wine lovers, while at the same time widening the spread of his clientele.

Rose Sainte-Croix (Château)

Commune: Listrac-Médoc. **Proprietor:** Monsieur Philippe Porcheron. Vineyard manager and cellar master: Monsieur Roger Porcheron. Consultant oenologist: Jacques Boissenot, Lamarque. **Size of vineyard:** 12 hectares. **Average age of vines:** 22 years. **Varieties:** 37% cabernet, 60% merlot, 3% petit-verdot. **Production:** 50 *tonneaux,* 60,000 bottles CB. **Visits:** Saturdays from 8 a.m. to 6 p.m. or by appointment, tel.56 58 14 24 . **Direct sales and by mail order:** in France. Château Rose Sainte-Croix, Listrac-Médoc, 33480 Castelnau-de-Médoc.

The wine of Rose Sainte-Croix is good even in off-years.

During the Napoleonic wars, the soldier Buroleau fought bravely. In recognition of his sterling and loyal service to the nation in the ranks of the army, the state gave him some land situated in Listrac, in the region called Donissan. Buroleau wasted no time; he thanked the Emperor and hurried off to plant vines. That was in 1812. Château Rose Sainte-Croix is the result of this gift and for many years the Buroleaus, father and son, were active among the small proprietors of Listrac. Then one of the Buroleau daughters married Jean-Pierre Laurent, who continued his in-laws' 150-year-old family tradition of vine-growing. But for reasons of health he sold up in 1986, and the estate found a new owner in the person of Philippe Porcheron, a builder from Moulis. It is his father, Roger Porcheron, who is principally in charge of the estate.

Rose Saint-Croix is a classic Listrac with the four traditional Médoc varieties here adapted to the land of each different parcel. A gold medal won in 1972 proves its ability (like many Listracs) to hold up well even in off-years. The château sells direct at reasonable prices which are particulary attractive for some vintages. Relatively well-rounded and aromatic, this wine is characterized by moderate levels of tannins and is seldom aggressive even in its youth. The 82s, 83s and 85s have now fully opened up. They do not boast an overpowering personality, but nevertheless, like all the more recent vintages, display an honest level of quality and are supple and pleasant. Wine lovers should reserve a few bottles in *primeur* every year.

The Porcherons are not only viticulturalists, they are also poets, as these four lines of their own composition testify:

"Our foremost concern and our greatest reward
Is to satisfy you and your guests. This we swear!
And contented we'll be if we hear all declare
That a wine fit for kings reigns supreme at your board."

Ruat Petit Poujeaux (Château)

Commune: Moulis-en-Médoc. **Proprietor:** Pierre Goffre-Viaud. Consultant oenologist: CBC, Libourne. **Size of vineyard:** 14 hectares. **Average age of vines:** 10 years. **Varieties:** 40% cabernet-sauvignon, 15% cabernet-franc, 45% merlot. **Production:** 90,000 bottles. **Visits:** Pierre Goffre-Viaud, tel. 57 51 11 97. **Direct sales and by mail order:** in France. Pierre Goffre-Viaud, 11 rue Giraud, 33500 Libourne. **Marketing:** 90% through the trade.

The Goffres were growers in the little locality of Petit-Poujeaux in Moulis right at the beginning of the nineteenth century. As for the Viauds, they settled there on October 21, 1871, "with the right to use the name of Château Ruat, for which purpose the property's one and only branding stamp has been handed to them." Pierre Goffre-Viaud represents the perfect synthesis of these two lines today, both in his name and in his wine. The *cru* is currently undergoing reconstruction and he hopes to have sixteen hectares under production in the very near future. The vineyard is situated in the heart of Moulis in two parcels with more or less similar soil – upper Eocene limestone, such as is found in Saint-Estèphe and neighbouring Listrac.

With two hectares of cabernet-franc and the rest split equally between merlot and cabernet-sauvignon, Pierre Goffre-Viaud does not make a wine which is easily compared with the work of other growers. He harvests as late as possible, when the grapes are beginning to become over-ripe. Then he vinifies at a high temperature and bottles rapidly. In other words, the wine does not spend much time in wood. This early bottling means the wine can keep its fruitiness and develop a bouquet rather quickly without too much acidity or astringency. Because of this, Ruat Petit Poujeaux soon attains an elegant roundness and does not need to be kept for ten years to be enjoyed.

Saransot-Dupré (Château)

Commune: Listrac-Médoc. **Proprietor:** Yves Raymond. Vineyard manager: Guy Larché. Cellar master: Xavier Barennes. Consultant oenologist: Bernard Couasnon, Pauillac. **Size of a vineyard:** 11.5 hectares. **Average age of vines:** 20 years. **Varieties:** 40% cabernet-sauvignon, 60% merlot. **Production:** 50 *tonneaux*, 60,000 bottles CB. **Visits:** daily except Sunday. Tel. 56 58 03 02. **Direct sales and by mail order:** Château Saransot-Dupré, Listrac-Médoc, 33480 Castelnau-de-Médoc. **Marketing:** through the trade.

Just as Fonréaud owes its name to a fountain, Saransot-Dupré owes its to a stream. It is only the tiniest of streams but it crosses the estate, winding down Le

Saransot-Dupré's excellent wine is enjoyed by customers and neighbours alike.

Tris towards Les Marcieux, where it flows into another stream, equally modest but with the swashbuckling name of Gartaillon. Formerly, when Saransot's final "t" was pronounced (in the manner of Turandot), the word was used for the rivulets by the side of the fields, vineyards and meadows in the Gironde, and many of these can be found on the local land registers. Saransot quite naturally took the additional name of Dupré, which also appears at Fourcas. In 1843 Adolphe Dupré, a solicitor in Bordeaux, bought the two estates of Fourcas and Saransot, at that time united and known by the name of Cru Roulet. They had formerly belonged to Marie-Nicole de Saint-Géran, the widow of a knight of the Order of Saint-Louis called Jean-Louis Hostein-Duffort, who had inherited a substantial part of the estates from a certain Jean-Pierre Hostein, a lawyer in Bordeaux, who bought the estate with its cellar on May 8, 1735 from Pierre Carrasset, through the "royal notary", the esteemed Maître Bernon. So Saransot's vineyard, cited in this legal document, has existed since the beginning of the eighteenth century, or even before. This long life seems to have had an effect on the wine, which matures so well that you have the impression that it does not age at all. But to return to Adolphe Dupré: he was the more pleased at coming to Listrac because his brother Jean-Baptiste (nicknamed Chéri!) already cultivated vines on the nearby land of Marcilhanet in Saint-Laurent. In Adolphe's hands Cru Roulet became one of the leading wines of the commune, and in about 1850 the lawyer-grower was valiantly producing one hundred *tonneaux* a year.

However, on his death in 1875, his heirs fell out among themselves and once again the properties were put up for sale. It was Ovide Raymond, son of a teacher in the commune and member of one of the oldest families in Listrac, who bought them for 400,000 francs. The Raymonds already had a tradition of vine-growing for they worked a few rows which were known in the nineteenth century by the name of *cru* Guilhem-de-Louisot. Unfortunately for them, the end of the century brought in its train a series of crises: mildew, phylloxera and other natural disasters wreaked havoc on the estate. Ovide Raymond had to dispose of Fourcas, which was bought at auction for 93,000 francs by Jules-Victor Cathala. But he retained Saransot, which has remained in the family ever since. After Ovide, his son Darius, his grandson Philippe and today his great-grandson Yves have taken charge of the estate, which comprises 12 hectares of vines planted mainly in land of chalky clay. 169

Because of its size, its soil, its choice of vines and the quality of its wine, Saransot-Dupré is entirely typical of its appellation. It has a long-established reputation in Belgium where it is distributed by the little *négociant* business created by Philippe Raymond after the war. the estate is also unusual in producing a white wine, so remaining faithful to a practice which at one time was quite normal in the commune, though now generally abandoned. Formerly in Listrac there were many white wines, including Merle Blanc (Clarke), La Mouette or Le Cygne.

CHATEAU

SARANSOT-DUPRÉ

LISTRAC·MEDOC

Despite these attractive ornithological names, they have disappeared one by one. Yves Raymond still produces his white wine, vinified in the cask and sold by the same name as his red but with the Bordeaux appellation. We know that the number of producers of white wine in the Médoc can be numbered on the fingers of two hands and that they form a select group. Do not be afraid to ask Yves Raymond for a few bottles of this well-made but as yet barely known white wine. But that should not stop you sampling his red too. Firm and well-tructured, Saransot-Dupré can appear austere in its early youth, but once it has begun to age it develops a remarkable bouquet and lingers in the palate. Certain old vintages are still staggering, a sign of an amazing suitability for ageing. It is always reliable and worth having in your cellar.

Sémeillan (Château)

Commune: Listrac-Médoc. **Proprietor:** GFA Sémeillan. Director: Madame Sauterel. Vineyard manager: Régis Martin. **Size of vineyard:** 13 hectares. **Average age of vines:** approx. 40 years. **Varieties:** 80% cabernet-sauvignon, 20% merlot. **Production:** 50 *tonneaux*. **Visits:** by appointment. Régis Martin. Tel. 56 58 01 03. **Direct sales and by mail order:** in France and abroad. Château Sémeillan, Listrac-Médoc, 33480 Castelnau-de-Médoc.

There is every reason to believe that the name of Sémeillan comes from the name of the vine-stock "sémillon", a white wine variety once cultivated in the Médoc and still very common in the Gironde, particularly in Sauternes. Historically, the study of such names is interesting for sometimes it reveals one the very opposite of what might expect. Take, for example, the Pontacs, an important family of growers in previous centuries, who gave their name to a vine, the pontac, grown today in South Africa.

Château Sémeillan has a long history. Under the Ancien Régime it is said to have belonged to Marshal de Richelieu (see Duplessis-Fabre). In the nineteenth century Napoleon III agreed to be godfather to one of the children of the proprietor of the day, a Monsieur Bonnet, for he was particularly fond of this *cru*. The influence of emperors on vineyards is something which should not be underestimated. Napoleon I, for example, was in the region of Blaye during 1809. While he and

170

his entourage were travelling through the village of Marsas, on the way to Spain, the Empress was seized with a pressing need. The procession halted and without further ado, France's first lady squatted among the vines in answer to nature's call. Naturally the news soon spread everywhere and was the cause of general merriment among the locals, especially because the parcel of vines which had received this august visit was named on the land register as "Congaillard" which is untranslatable in a respectable publication. Today, the proprietor of this land has turned the event to good account, and under the name of "La pissotière de l'impératrice" ("The empress's pisspot") produces an unpretentious Bordeaux Supérieur whose name alone is worth the price of the bottle.

Château Sémeillan also belonged to Pierre Balleux, a Listrac personality before the war. Estate manager of Fourcas Hosten, Gressier Grand Poujeaux, Fourcas Dupré and his own *cru* all at the same time, he used to travel from one to the other by bicycle and managed to direct everything perfectly with an authority no-one dared to challenge. His daughter married Armand Faulat, the last mayor of Caudéran before it was incorporated into Bordeaux itself. Then the property was owned by Henri Bibian, another local figure from an old growing family and mayor of Listrac until 1983. He replanted the best land on either side of the main road on the way into the village. The present owner, Madame Sauterel, of Swiss origin, has continued renovating, but only inside the château. For the upkeep of the vineyard is not entirely satisfactory. The once-good reputation of this *cru* does not deserve this neglect which we hope will be short-lived.

Sémeillan-Mazeau (Château) ♟♟♟♟♟

Commune: Listrac-Médoc. **Proprietor:** Family GFA Sémeillan-Mazeau. Manager: Hervé Mazeau. Vineyard manager and cellar master: Alain Bistodeau. Consultant oenologist: Jacques Boissenot, Lamarque. **Size of vineyard:** 11 hectares. **Average age of vines:** 20 years. **Varieties:** 50% cabernet-sauvignon, 50% merlot. **Production:** 55 *tonneaux*, 30,000 bottles CB. **Visits:** from June 1 to September 15, Monday to Friday, from 8.30 a.m. to 12.30 p.m. Groups by appointment. Monsieur Bistodeau, tel. 56 58 01 12. **Direct sales and by mail order:** in France and abroad. SCE Sémeillan-Mazeau, Listrac-Médoc, 33480 Castelnau-de-Médoc. **Marketing:** through the trade.

The memory of Joseph Mazeau, the former president of the Viticultural Federation of Listrac, is still very much alive in the village. At once the estate manager of Fonréaud and owner of this *cru,* which he had acquired through his in-laws, he fought tooth and nail for Listrac's right to become an independent appellation, a goal which he achieved in 1955. Thirty years later it became "appellation Listrac-Médoc contrôlée", an extra precaution to avoid all possible confusion with the wines of Lirac. Joseph Mazeau well deserves his reputation as a grower in Listrac, and it is only right that one of the good *crus* in the commune should perpetuate a respected name.

Château Sémeillan-Mazeau was originally a major part of Château Sémeillan which belonged at the beginning of the century to Vicomtesse du Cheyron du Pavillon and at that time was one of the largest producers in Listrac. It then passed into the hands of Monsieur Hostein, whose three daughters became Madame Balleux,

Madame Henri Bibian and Madame Joseph Mazeau. In 1938, this family trust led to the creation of a second Sémeillan which today is in the hands of Mazeau family, as a private GFA created in 1979 and a private company of which Hervé Mazeau is manager.

Tour de Laulan 🍷

→ *Fourcas-Loubaney*

Tour Granins (Château) 🍷🍷🍷🍷🍷

Commune: Moulis-en-Médoc. **Proprietor:** Jean-Louis Telley. **Size of vineyard:** 6 hectares. **Visits:** tel. 56 58 04 52. **Direct sales:** Château Tour Granins, Moulis-en-Médoc, 33480 Castelnau-de-Médoc. **Marketing:** part sold to the trade in bulk.

Sold in bulk

The little vineyard of Tour Granins is related to that of Granins Grand Poujeaux. Until 1983, both belonged to Edouard Batailley, who had patiently grouped together twelve hectares of vines around Grand-Poujeaux. Tour Granins is now in the hands of Jean-Louis Telley, Monsieur Batailley's son-in-law, who has four parcels of land near Chasse-Spleen and Poujeaux, "land where the petit-verdot ripens well", as Edouard Batailley stresses. The new proprietor sells a large part of his harvest in bulk to the trade, but he keeps back a few bottles for visitors passing through Grand-Poujeaux. Tour Granins represents the amalgamation of two vineyards, that of Granins, formerly owned by the Lescoutras, and that of Peyredon. It could have called itself La Tour Granins if the famous Château Latour in Pauillac had not claimed (sometimes at law) a monopoly on the name, even when prefixing another. As a result of this determination to safeguard its name, more than two hundred growing estates throughout the world have been renamed. The majority, like Tour Granins, have been content simply to omit the word "La". Others have refused to submit and have been obliged to do so by legal sanctions. Up till now only one solitary wine has emerged the winner from this battle: the celebrated La Tour Haut-Brion in the Passac-Léognan appellation.

Tourille (Château) 🍷🍷🍷🍷🍷

Commune: Listrac-Médoc. **Proprietor:** Madame Raspaud. **Size of vineyard:** 2 hectares. **Varieties:** 50% merlot, 50% cabernet-sauvignon. **Production:** 9,000 bottles CB. **Sales by mail order:** Château Tourille, Médrac, Listrac-Médoc, 33480 Castelnau-de-Médoc.

label not communicated

The cellar master at Chasse-Spleen for twenty years, Yves Raspaud was an exceptional man, good-natured, skilful and unpretentious. On Médrac's excellent gravelly soil he established a small *cru* – a wine which he made with loving care and which was snapped up by his friends. But out of natural modesty Yves Raspaud never

One of the region's famous personalities, Y. Raspaud made wine in his own image.

spoke of Tourille, which was his sort of secret garden. When he died in 1989, his colleagues and friends took the estate in hand and now it is Robert Chabet, the cultivation supervisor at Chasse-Spleen, who is tenant farmer. The wine receives the same care and attention, and vinification is still carried out in the traditional way, in accordance with the sound Médoc method which Yves Raspaud respected to the letter. Small in size, Château Tourille is great in stature thanks to the memory of its founder.

Tressan (Château de)

Commune: Moulis-en-Médoc. **Proprietor:** Monsieur Christian Prud'homme. Vineyard managers: Annie and Christian Prud'homme. Consultant oenologist: Jacques Boissenot, Lamarque. **Size of vineyard:** 5.75 hectares. **Average age of vines:** more than 50 years. **Varieties:** 36% cabernet-sauvignon, 15% cabernet-franc, 24% merlot, 25% petit-verdot. **Production:** 2.5 *tonneaux*. 5,000 bottles CB. **Visits:** by appointment. Annie and Christian Prud'homme, tel. 56 59 08 69. **Direct sales and by mail order:** in France and abroad. Château de Tressan, Moulis-en-Médoc, 33480 Castelnau-de-Médoc.

Christian Prud'homme had already brought Château Meyre at Avensan back to life when here in Moulis he created a new label, Château de Tressan. At one time its five hectares, planted with very old vines, formed part of the Graves de Guitignan belonging to Armand Goffre. Subsequently it was Charles Richebon who looked after the vines for more than thirty-five years, until he was 82. Then Christian Prud'homme, a wine enthusiast, took on this modest estate situated on good Quaternary gravel. He is also proprietor of a little vineyard by the railway in Cantenac. If you want to discover an unknown Moulis, write to Annie or Christian Prud'homme.

Veyrin (Château)

→ Donissan

Vieux Moulin (Château)

Commune: Listrac-Médoc. **Proprietor:** Madame Dufau and Mademoiselle Fort, Le Tris, Listrac-Médoc, 33480 Castelnau-de-Médoc. **Size of vineyard:** 5.5 hectares. **Average age of vines:** 20 years. **Varieties:** 47% cabernet-sauvignon, 38% merlot, 15% petit-verdot. **Production:** 20 *tonneaux*. 24,000 bottles CB. **Marketing:** vinified at the *Cave de vinification* at Listrac, tel. 56 58 03 19.

Although it consists of only a few hectares, Vieux Moulin is the result of the amalgamation of three estates. The first was once called Clos du Colonel, the second belonged to Léopold Fort and the third to Paul Bosq, one of the founders of the *coopérative* in 1935. His heirs run this little estate today, with vines on either side of the main road to the north of Listrac. The wine is vinified at the *coopérative*, but has retained its own label. The medals won by recent vintages prove that the estate is in good hands.

Annexes

Other growers in Moulis and Listrac registering harvest return figures.

BEGU, Fernand   0.5 hectares
Moulis-en-Médoc, 33480 Castelnau

FILHASTRE, Christian   0.48 hectares
Médrac, Listrac-Médoc, 33480 Castelnau

GRAMOND, Moïse   1 hectare
Donissan, Listrac-Médoc, 33480 Castelnau

MALEYRAN, Suzanne   0.5 hectares
Moulis-en-Médoc, 33480 Castelnau

MILLET, Pierre   0.8 hectares
Clos Martinon, Listrac-Médoc,
33480 Castelnau

PIAT, René   0.7 hectares
Château Lacour, Bouqueyran,
Moulis-en-Médoc, 33480 Castelnau

RANCINANGUE, Pierre   0.55 hectares
Moulis-en-Médoc,
33480 Castelnau

Members of the Cave coopérative of Listrac-Médoc

AMBACH, Henriette   0.56 hectares
Le Bourg, Listrac-Médoc,
33480 Castelnau

ARNAUD, Michel   2.5 hectares
La Herreyre, Avensan, 33480 Castelnau

BACQUEY, Maurice   2.01 hectares
Libardac, Listrac-Médoc, 33480 Castelnau

BARTHELEMY, Jean   1.17 hectares
Lambert, Listrac-Médoc, 33480 Castelnau

BEGU, Denise   3.8 hectares
Peymasson, Moulis-en-Médoc, 33480 Castelnau

BLANC, André   7.73 hectares
Le Bourg, Listrac-Médoc, 33480 Castelnau

BLANC, Pierre   0.73 hectares
Le Haut, Avensan, 33480 Castelnau

BOUSCARRUT, Gérard   0.88 hectares
Moulis-en-Médoc, 33480 Castelnau

CAMIN, Roland   2.0 hectares
Le Montaud, Listrac-Médoc, 33480 Castelnau

CASTEL, Pierre   4.21 hectares
Donissan, Listrac-Médoc, 33480 Castelnau

CHAUMON, Marcel   1.68 hectares
Le Bourg, Listrac-Médoc, 33480 Castelnau

CHEVALIER, Michel   5.13 hectares
Berniquet, Listrac-Médoc, 33480 Castelnau

CHEVALIER, Robert   3.52 hectares
Berniquet, Listrac-Médoc, 33480 Castelnau

COUNAUD, Hubert   1.45 hectares
Le Bourg, Listrac-Médoc, 33480 Castelnau

DAURAT, Jean   4.18 hectares
Libardac, Listrac-Médoc, 33480 Castelnau

DAVID, Gérard   2.35 hectares
Libardac, Listrac-Médoc, 33480 Castelnau

DE FRETTES, Pierre   5.62 hectares
Berniquet, Listrac-Médoc, 33480 Castelnau

DUBET, Christian   0.61 hectares
Le Tris, Listrac-Médoc, 33480 Castelnau

EYQUEM, Alain   0.8 hectares
Le Temple, 33680 Lacanau

EYQUEM, Clément   2.91 hectares
Donissan, Listrac-Médoc, 33480 Castelnau

FAUX, André   0.66 hectares
Berniquet, Listrac-Médoc, 33480 Castelnau

FERNANDEZ, Maxime   1.5 hectares
Petit-Poujeaux, Moulis-en-Médoc,
33480 Castelnau

GAEC LESCOUTRA-MIQUAU
    22.63 hectares
Moulin du Bourg, Listrac-Médoc,
33480 Castelnau

HOCHGENUG, Philippe   1.19 hectares
Médrac, Moulis-en-Médoc, 33480 Castelnau

HOSTEIN, Pierre   0.03 hectares
Le Bourg, Listrac-Médoc, 33480 Castelnau

HOSTENS, Michel   1.68 hectares
Moulin de Laborde, Listrac-Médoc, 33480
Castelnau

HOSTENS, Roger   1.5 hectares
Libardac, Listrac-Médoc, 33480 Castelnau

HOSTENS, Roland   4.4 hectares
Donissan, Listrac-Médoc, 33480 Castelnau

JOINIS, Roger (Mme)   0.16 hectares
La Barreyre, Listrac-Médoc,
33480 Castelnau

LABATUT, Jean and ANTOLDI, Franck
0.81 hectares
Grand-Poujeaux, Moulis-en-Médoc,
33480 Castelnau

LACOTTE, Huguette   1.71 hectares
Gayon, Listrac-Médoc, 33480 Castelnau

LAJOUX, Jean-Louis   1.45 hectares
Le Bourg, Listrac-Médoc, 33480 Castelnau

LESCOUTRA, André   0.73 hectares
Brach, 33480 Castelnau

LESCOUTRA, Jean   4.26 hectares
Libardac, Listrac-Médoc, 33480 Castelnau

LESTAGE, Marc   4.64 hectares
Moulis-en-Médoc, 33480 Castelnau

MALEYRAN, Guy   2.4 hectares
Le Meynieu, Brach, 33480 Castelnau

MALEYRAN, Max   4.32 hectares
Le Bourg, Listrac-Médoc, 33480 Castelnau

MARRACO, Manuel   4.01 hectares
Bardouillan, 33112 Saint-Laurent-et-Benon

MARTIN, Edgar   2 hectares
Montaud, Listrac-Médoc, 33480 Castelnau

MEYRE, Jean-Guy   0.59 hectares
33112 Saint-Laurent-et-Benon

MEYRE, Pierre-Paul   0.97 hectares
Barbat, Listrac-Médoc, 33480 Castelnau

MOURRAUT, Pierre   1.27 hectares
Larousse, 33112 Saint-Laurent-et-Benon

NAULEAU, Marie-Louise   2.34 hectares
Touleron, Listrac-Médoc, 33480 Castelnau

PETIT, Raoul   2.46 hectares
Chaux, Moulis-en-Médoc, 33480 Castelnau

POITOU, Jean-Pierre   1.35 hectares
Pontet, Listrac-Médoc, 33480 Castelnau

PONTET, Marie-Jeanne   0.54 hectares
Codres, Listrac-Médoc, 33480 Castelnau

PORCHERON, Christian   0.29 hectares
Lieulet, Moulis-en-Médoc, 33480 Castelnau

PORCHERON, Roger   2.16 hectares
Lieulet, Moulis-en-Médoc, 33480 Castelnau

RANCINANGUE, Jean   0.89 hectares
Barbat, Listrac-Médoc, 33480 Castelnau

RAYMOND, André   1.84 hectares
Donissan, Listrac-Médoc, 33480 Castelnau

RAYMOND, David   0.41 hectares
Ludeye, Listrac-Médoc, 33480 Castelnau

RAYMOND, Francis   0.66 hectares
Le Grand Ludeye, Sainte-Hélène,
33480 Castelnau

RAYMOND, Hector   1.31 hectares
Berniquet, Listrac-Médoc, 33480 Castelnau

RAYMOND, Henri   1.55 hectares
Donissan, Listrac-Médoc, 33480 Castelnau

RAYMOND, Jean-Marie   8.42 hectares
Ludeye, Listrac-Médoc, 33480 Castelnau

RAYMOND, Michel   0.36 hectares
Le Bourg, Listrac-Médoc, 33480 Castelnau

RICHEBON, Paul   4.13 hectares
Petit-Poujeaux, Moulis-en-Médoc,
33480 Castelnau

RICHEBON-PERNET (Family trust)
0.53 hectares
Petit-Poujeaux, Moulis-en-Médoc,
33480 Castelnau

SAINTOUT, Jean-Paul   2.34 hectares
Devidas, 33112 Saint-Laurent-et-Benon

SAUTS, Frères   3.17 hectares
Donissan, Listrac-Médoc, 33480 Castelnau

SAUX, Guy   0.55 hectares
Le Bourg, Listrac-Médoc, 33480 Castelnau

SCE FORT BOSC   4.39 hectares
Le Tris, Listrac-Médoc, 33480 Castelnau

SCEA AGRICOLE DE CARTUJAC
3.74 hectares
Bruno Saintout, 33112 Saint-Laurent-et-Benon

SERVY, Marie-Louise   4.62 hectares
Rue Georges-Mandel, 33480 Castelnau

SOCIETE MEYRE (Maurice and Philippe)
7.17 hectares
Donissan, Listrac-Médoc, 33480 Castelnau

SOUBRET, Jean   0.30 hectares
Libardac, Listrac-Médoc, 33480 Castelnau

VIAUT, Marie-Germaine   0.33 hectares
Le Bourg, Listrac-Médoc, 33480 Castelnau

VIDALLER, François   2.49 hectares
Barbat, Listrac-Médoc, 33480 Castelnau

VIDALLER, Jean-Bernard   1.59 hectares
Moulis-en-Médoc, 33480 Castelnau

VIDEAU, Lucienne   1 hectare
La Potence, 33480 Castelnau

YUSTEDE, Emile   0.64 hectares
Avensan, 33480 Castelnau

A different perspective

Pierre Chaveau is an artist who works in the old-fashioned way, with patience and care. His maps of the Bordeaux vineyards, starting on the left bank of the River Garonne and the estuary of the Gironde, are accompanied in this series by texts written by Bernard Ginestet. By courtesy of Editions du Ponant in Bordeaux, we here reproduce in small scale the maps of the Moulis and Listrac appellations, which find a natural place in this book (*Bordeaux Rive Gauche*, Bordeaux 1987).

Grapes and corn

Deep in colour, full-bodied, supple and with a fine bouquet, the wines of Moulis are natural and pure, delightfully fresh and round. They have some of the qualities of a Rubens painting: a bucolic canvas in soft and delectable flesh-tones. Moulis is an appellation apart, lying within the Médoc. It is not my part of the world but I know it well. For many years I watched carts, wagons and carriages, bringing wine, wood, flour, cattle and people ready to embark at Cussac or Lamarque, Soussans or Margaux. There was no parade of wealth, but everything was trim and neat, washed and ironed, from snow-white sheep to smart Sunday hats. Moulis typified absolute modesty. I imagined then great family wardrobes of gleaming oak or polished cherry containing linen scented with citronella: sheets dried in the open meadows, lace head-dresses, linen shirts. I know that in the shops the shelves were piled high with provisions to last the season through – duchesse pears, apples, black puddings, hams, potted meats, bacon, rabbit pâtés and foie gras. I believed that in the kitchens, not far from the simmering stockpot, the grandfather clock with its carefully regulated pendulum (the heartbeat of the household) concealed piles of louis d'or, a family secret handed down from generation to generation.

Moulis's beautiful church in its superbly sober style dates from the time of the Knights Templar. The centuries have passed, but the genius of the builders of these sanctuaries has remained, modified here and there by restorers or perfectionists. But the choir is intact. The capitals, the friezes and the bas-reliefs bear witness to the fervour of these religious artists. Here can be seen the story of Genesis, the earthly Paradise, Adam and Eve innocent and naked, the serpent of Evil, the bread and the wine of the sacrament symbolized by grapes and corn, the hare and the hound, man and the birds which alight on his head to teach him the language of Heaven. There is a profusion of scallop-shells, proving that originally the church here at Moulis was a resting point on the pilgrims' route to Compostella. And there are stone ornaments sculpted by a highly skilled chisel, in a style reminiscent of the early Christian church of the east.

In the Gascon tongue moulin *(mill) is pronounced "moolee", and in the plural "mooleex". We need look no further for the origin of the name. For Moulis was a land of millers, who very early on chose their preferred spots. Two principal streams, the Barbot and the Moulis, wind their way through charming valleys, and their steady flow used to turn the millwheels which ground the corn. Along their shady banks are drifts of columbine, periwinkle, milkwort and the lesser centaury (the millers' daughters looked so pretty as they gathered them by the armful). But water power was not the only way of making flour. Windmills spread their white sails on the hilltops. The west wind, which sometimes blows with tremendous force, was harnessed by the millers on the higher land. The water-millers called the windmillers* pauvres girouettes *("wretched weathercocks"), and in return were mocked as* petites lavettes ("little drips"). *All ran their lives according to the rhythms of wind or water, flood or drought, calm or storm. Then, one day, a water-miller began to plant vines rising up the slope just as a windmiller was planting some from the top. Thus they joined together, gaining mutual respect. Since then the millers of Moulis have become vine growers. The grapes and the corn engraved on their church commemorate the union. For wine proved a stronger force than either wind or water.*

The vineyards of Moulis ▶

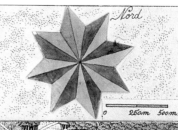

Controlée du Médoc
LIS

Nord

0   250m   500m

Grand Poujeaux

28

26 27
25
24
23 22 20
19 18
17

15

14

12
Poujeaux

16

Bouqueyran   5 Mauvesin   6 La Mouline
Ruat   11 Biston Brillette 12 Guitignan
Brillette   17 Cru les Graves   18 Gressier Gd Poujeaux
Dutruch Gd Poujeaux 23 La Closerie   24 Robert Franquet
Poujeaux   28 Maucaillou

CONCEPTION et DESSIN: Pierre CHAVEAU.
© 1983 TOUS DROITS RÉSERVÉS

A assertive flavour

Listrac is the "far west" of the vine-growing Médoc. There are three main types of people in the peninsula – the ribeyrins, *who are my neighbours on the river; the* grabeyrans, *the people from the gravelly lands; and the* landescots, *those from the moors. Traditionally, the Ribeyrin has the reputation of being nitpicking and often wily by nature. The Grabeyran is proud and jealous of his wine. The Landescot is taciturn, tight-fisted but warm-hearted. The people of Listrac belong to both of these two last types, so forming an original ethnic group deeply in love with their land. On the lips of a Grabeyran, the term Landescot is pejorative (*landerou *means "lazy") but the Landescot will quickly retort "pathetic Grabeyran". The community of Listrac has had to learn to live together. And, undoubtedly because of this, it displays two outstanding characteristics: tolerance and hospitality. Today these traits are beginning to disappear. There is perhaps less local colour than before, but the picture still retains its original outlines and shading. Though faded by time and worn by change, the image can still be seen, like a cask which has not been filled for many years but which still retains the smell of wine.*

The village is large, lying on a gravelly ridge stretching along the main road from Bordeaux to the Pointe de Grave, and surrounded by vineyards forming a huge clearing on an undulating landscape. The forest describes a protective circle rather like a fruit tart, widening as it stretches into the distance, and cut into slices to create roads. The resulting star shape is an indication that Listrac has always enjoyed good relations with its neighbours. Today people come here from all over the world for the pleasure of buying good wine. For the wine of Listrac is dependable and well-structured, brawny but not coarse. Better to relish its straight forward freshness than to ponder the elegant delicacy of a more distinguished wine. No, you will not find a precious, aristocratic language here, nor an affected snobbery. But you will find a cheering bottle which speaks with its hands, making sweeping gestures of friendship. A friendly slap on the back from a good Listrac is better than all the caresses of a pretentious cru *("sword-thrusts, gentlemen, sword-thrusts, not pin-pricks!" as Tartarin would have said). Very often, the rugged accents of the land hide a wealth of sensitivity in which country wisdom turns into philosophy. The dialect of Listrac has its own subtleties.*

The two great diversions in Listrac are hunting and gathering the mushrooms known as ceps. The area covered by the commune is extensive and migratory birds rest here on their journey. On the gravelly plateaux hunters lie in wait for flocks of larks which they catch in nets called "pantes". The hunter himself is called a "pantayre". In the woods and copses near the fairy rings of chanterelles woodcock are to be found in the last days of autumn and all through winter. It is traditional for the last ceps to be eaten with the first woodcock. As he returns home with his gun on his shoulder and his dog behind him, the triumphant Listrac hunter will have a handful of the last ceps in his left pocket and a woodcock in his right: a meal fit for a king, with an old

Listrac wine. He will happily reveal where he downed his woodcock, but will breathe not a word about where he gathered the ceps; they do not travel. Once the Listrac foresters used to walk about on stilts: perfect for spotting ceps, but hardly practical for gathering them.

The vineyards of Listrac ▶

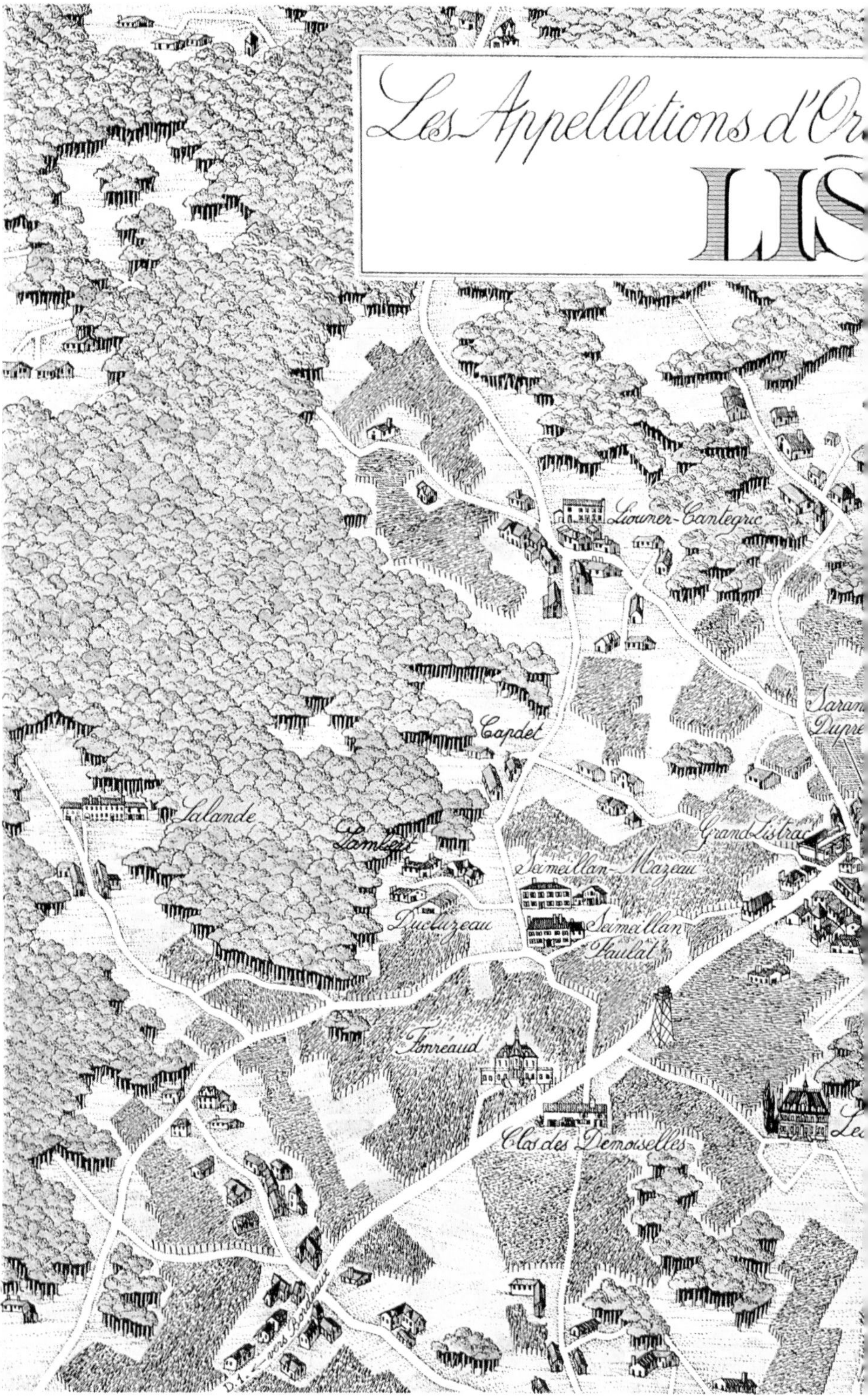

Les Appellations d'Or...
LIS

Liouner-Cantegric

Capdet

Saran
Dupre

Salande

Lamaou

Grand Listrac

Seimeillan-Mazeau

Ductazeau

Seimeillan
Faulat

Fonreaud

Clos des Demoiselles

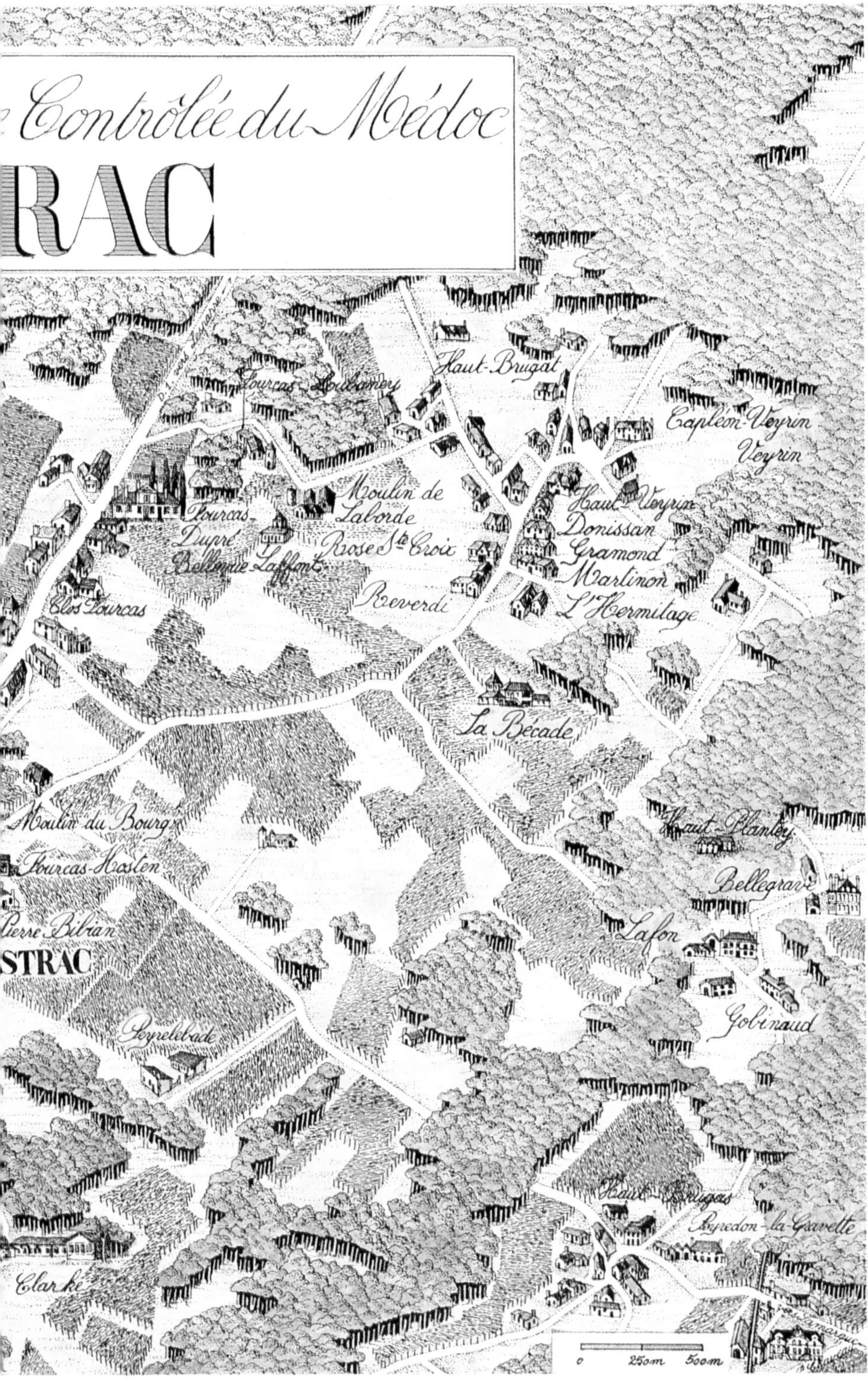

Contrôlée du Médoc

RAC

Fourcas Adcoubanne Haut-Brugat

Capléon-Veyrin
Veyrin

Moulin de
Laborde
Fourcas   Rose Ste Croix
Dupré
Bellevue Laffont

Haut-Veyrin
Donissan
Gramond
Martinon
L'Hermitage

Clos Fourcas   Reverdi

La Bécade

Moulin du Bourg   Haut-Planley

Fourcas-Hosten   Bellegrave

Pierre Bibian

STRAC   Lafon

Peynelabrade   Gobinaud

Haut-Bouygues
Peyredon-la-Gravette

Clarke

0   250m   500m

Index of proprietors

Picture acknowledgements:
All the photographs in this book are by *Luc Joubert, Bordeaux,* except those reproduced by kind permission of: Airlec, Aéroport de Mérignac (56, 62, 108); Château
Fonréaud (118); Château Lestage (141); Château Moulis (155); M. Porcheron
(167); Réunion des Musées Nationaux (75, 76, 88); Scope (Michel Guillard: 12,
16); Vinissimo (CFEE), Bordeaux (15).